# The Eye of Faith
## *A Practical Application of Bible Principles*

### Dr. Avis D. Hendrickson

**TEACH Services, Inc.**
P U B L I S H I N G
www.TEACHServices.com • (800) 367-1844

# The Eye of Faith
## A Practical Application of Biblical Principles

*A New Perspective on Life*
*(A Thankful Heart—from Dissatisfaction to Contentment)*

World rights reserved. This book or any portion thereof may not be copied or reproduced in any form or manner whatever, except as provided by law, without the written permission of the publisher, except by a reviewer who may quote brief passages in a review.

The author assumes full responsibility for the accuracy of all facts and quotations as cited in this book. The opinions expressed in this book are the author's personal views and interpretations, and do not necessarily reflect those of the publisher.

This book is provided with the understanding that the publisher is not engaged in giving spiritual, legal, medical, or other professional advice. If authoritative advice is needed, the reader should seek the counsel of a competent professional.

Copyright © 2019 Dr. Avis Hendrickson
Copyright © 2019 TEACH Services, Inc.
ISBN-13: 978-1-4796-0941-3 (Paperback)
ISBN-13: 978-1-4796-0944-4 (ePub)
Library of Congress Control Number: 2019911760

Scriptural references are from the King James Version of the Bible. Public domain.

*John 15:7—If ye abide in me, and my words abide in you, ye shall ask what ye will, and it shall be done unto you.*

# Table of Contents

**Prelude—Mother at War** .................................................. 9
**Foreword** ................................................................ 12
**About the Author** ....................................................... 15
    "Education is the Key ... to Opportunities" ..................... 15
**Preface** ................................................................ 24
**Introduction** ........................................................... 26
**A New Perspective on Life** ............................................. 27
    Every Day You Make Choices:
        Define the Basis for Your Choice ....................... 29
    Change Is Interesting. Who Takes Responsibility for It? ........ 32
    Framing Your Advancement ....................................... 34
    A Perspective on Your Value .................................... 35
**Personal Development** .................................................. 39
    The First Element of Wellness Is Spiritual ..................... 43
    The Second Element of Wellness Is Emotional .................... 46
    The Third Element of Wellness Is Intellectual .................. 48
    A Renewing of Your Mind. What Are You Thinking? ................ 51
    What Value Have You Placed on Time Managements?
        It Is Essential to Personal Development ................ 52
    The Fourth Element of Wellness Is Physical ..................... 54
**Lifestyle Management** .................................................. 56
    The Fifth Element of Wellness Is Social ........................ 56
    A New Perspective on Life—Representation
        What You Do Always Counts ............................. 57
    Parenting ...................................................... 63
    Personal Application ........................................... 64
    Implementation of a Nurturing Standard ......................... 65
    Parenting Through the Different Stages of Development
        (Parenting 101) ........................................ 65

Some Characteristics of the Stages of Development:
  Age, Phase, and Christian Nurturing Activities . . . . . . . . . . . . 67
The Sixth Element of Wellness Is Finance. . . . . . . . . . . . . . . . . . 72
A New Perspective on Wealth . . . . . . . . . . . . . . . . . . . . . . . . . . . . 74
A New Perspective on Life: When You Have a J.O.B. . . . . . . . . . . 78
The Seventh Element of Wellness Is Sexual . . . . . . . . . . . . . . . . . 80
A New Perspective on Love. . . . . . . . . . . . . . . . . . . . . . . . . . . . . . 80
In Reflection . . . . . . . . . . . . . . . . . . . . . . . . . . . . . . . . . . . . . . . . . 82

**Bibliography** . . . . . . . . . . . . . . . . . . . . . . . . . . . . . . . . . . . . . . . . . . . 85

# *Prelude—Mother at War*

*Psalm 35:18—I will give thee thanks in the great congregation:
I will praise thee among much people.*

Bombarded by acts of distress, emotional upheaval, and threats to my peace, quietude, physical wellbeing, privacy, and material possessions, I would cry, feel vulnerable, unsafe, helpless, and alone. Who do I ask for help? It can't be anyone I love. I don't want to put them in harm's way.

The social context of the times found me still in my parents' home, under their rules, during a period when society had gone awry: President John F. Kennedy assassinated; Rev. Dr. Martin Luther King, Jr. assassinated; Malcolm X assassinated. Who then can protect and take care of me? When even a person in the highest office in the United States, respected by the world, having immense authority, is killed, where is the safety?

In this social context, by the age of sixteen, I was married and a mother of one son. A few months into the marriage, my husband enlisted in the army and left for the Vietnam War—a decision he made without including me in the discussion, which may have taken place with others who influenced his decision. What a surprise!

Every sense of stability was disrupted. In our separation, I was robbed of the benefit of creating a state of affairs in my life that would mold and forge a refined family coexistence—like the *Adventures of Ozzie and Harriet* and *Father Knows Best* programs I watched on the black-and-white TV in the living room throughout my youth, or even like the relationships my mother and father, as well as my aunt and uncle, appeared to have with each other.

Some say there is good, bad, and ugly in life. By the age of sixteen, I had had experiences that were bad and seemed to border on ugly. The bad: I was molested; the good: I was saved from anything worse. The bad: I experienced pubic rejection; the good: I moved beyond the limitations that others imposed on me based on their perception of my circumstances. The bad: I was marginalized in my involvement in organizations; the good: I developed confidence.

By age sixteen, I had one child. By age thirty-one, I was the mother of four children with no apparent husband in sight. People who watched me move around with my children in tow would, by their behavior, say, 'Where does she think she's going?' I'm glad you asked. Fast forward: I've accomplished my goal of an improved lifestyle for myself and my family, without neglecting my responsibilities. I was able to move us forward while simultaneously enriching their development according to their stages in life.

I was more than what met the eye. By thirty-one, I had been married twice, obtained a master's degree in education, had a mortgage on a luxury co-op in which we lived, and held a professional position in an institution of higher education. "Life for me ain't been no crystal stair" (Langston Hughes, "Mother to Son").

I kept silent about my circumstances so that I had a clearer passage to accomplish my goal—a better lifestyle for my family and me. I learned that people talked. If I allowed their intrusion, their misguided and misplaced perceptions would further hinder my progression and create more unnecessary obstacles to overcome.

Along my path were affirmations of my silence. One day, early in my professional career in higher education, an African-American woman whom I looked up to as a mentor described her oldest son's relationship as "messy"—he had a child out of wedlock. She communicated his plight as a sense of untenable circumstances.

My own family relationship circumstances weren't husband and wife living together, cooperatively nurturing a family. I didn't want to provide information that would create a work environment that perceives me as less than whole in the relationship-and-family sphere. It would add additional layers of unnecessary stuff to overcome in my pursuit of recognition for advancement.

Later on, in a more advanced position reporting to a CEO in a predominantly white institution of higher education, I offered some insight as to why I was requesting a day off: "The ceiling in my bedroom fell, and it was going to be replaced."

Her reply: "Your life is full of calamities."

Affirmation: only share need-to-know information. In fairness, to put her statement in context, it is helpful to know that I told her sometime earlier that my husband had lung cancer and when necessary, I would be taking time off from work to accompany him to his doctor's appointments.

Only God made a way for me through acts of kindness from others and my conviction—confidence in the Holy Bible. Never be afraid to trust the unknown future to the all-knowing God. "We have nothing to fear for the future, except as we shall forget the way the Lord has led us, and His teaching in our past history" (White 1915, p. 196).

The pathway from the past indicates the way to the future. When Christians forget God's past leading, they also lose their sense of identity in the present, and that loss of identity causes a deficiency of mission and purpose. After all, if you don't know who you are in relation to God's plan, what do you have to tell the world?

At Mrs. Coretta Scott King's (MLK's widow) funeral, which I viewed on the television, Rev. Joseph Lowery, president of the Southern Christian Leadership Conference, said to Bernice King and the other children, "Know who you are and whose you are!"

> *When Christians forget God's past leading, they also lose their sense of identity in the present, and that loss of identity causes a deficiency of mission and purpose. After all, if you don't know who you are in relation to God's plan, what do you have to tell the world?*

# Foreword

Thank you, God, for loving me! This love experience is fulfilling; wholly satisfying. Your love gives me an elated state of being. It is the best I've ever experienced and imagined. You treat me so well, whatever condition I'm in. Your acts of love are always appropriate for my situation, as well as elevating.

In return, Dear God, I want to follow the former demoniac's example: "Howbeit Jesus suffered him not, but said unto him, Go home to thy friends, and tell them how great things the Lord hath done for thee, and hath had compassion on thee. And he departed, and began to publish in Decapolis how great things Jesus had done for him: and all *men* did marvel" (Mark 5:19, 20).

This writing is intended to contribute to a frame of reference for lifestyle management and personal development. The emphasis is on identifying boundaries and standards of living with the practical application of biblical principles. More to come at another time.

To provide an overview of lifestyle management and personal development, consider the mental imagery of a train to illustrate how we move through life. In New York City, up until about the 1970s, there was the Third Avenue El train, which traveled above ground and underground. Across much of the United States, AMTRAK and foreign countries' trains are in operation. They, for the most part, have two or more cars, which accommodate many passengers in sitting, standing, and sometimes sleeping. Every train moves along a train track, makes designated stops, and always takes longer than you want to travel to "your stop."

There's a variety of riders. Some of them get directions about the stop at which they should get off for their destination. Other riders just take a ride with no particular destination or goal. There are others who get distracted, either missing their stop or getting off somewhere other than their intended stop, out of curiosity or at the persuasion of someone who has their attention.

In some countries, trains stop running at a particular time, creating a missed opportunity when the schedule isn't followed. To get to a prescribed destination you should be intentional. Plan your work and work your plan, following God's guidance.

My journey to the high calling—"I press toward the mark for the prize of the high calling of God in Christ Jesus" (Philippians 3:14)—started blind. At my core, I knew there had to be a better way than the existence I was experiencing. Now I see and am growing in my clarity. As I travel, the blindness begins to dissipate, and enlightenment replaces portions of my impaired vision. I'm gaining more light as I press forward. I haven't arrived yet, but I know I'm not stuck in a place I symbolically characterized as an environment of cackling chickens. I embrace the atmosphere of eagles.

Like the illustration of the train, people travel daily and decide whether they're going to stop, pause, or continue to the next stop(s). Like a train ride, your decision will mold your personal development.

A transformation takes place with deliberate engagement in personal development. It means a difference in thinking and doing. It's not the same old dress, shoes, behaving, thinking, and doing. I've heard that the definition of insanity is doing the same thing and expecting different results. In Christ, you are a new creature; old things are passed away. There is a new birth of character, signifying being born again altogether. This change is lodged in the stronghold of your mind. What are you thinking? "Therefore if any man be in Christ, he is a new creature: old things are passed away; behold, all things are become new" (2 Corinthians 5:17).

> *A transformation takes place with deliberate engagement in personal development.*

Be faithful as you grow in understanding. Regardless of your age, starting fresh is like a child learning new principles. With commitment to practical biblical principles and practice, you successfully move through the stages of life. Be encouraged by these verses: "He hath shewed thee, O man, what is good; and what doth the Lord require of thee, but to do justly, and to love mercy, and to walk humbly with thy God" (Micah 6:8)? "His lord said unto him, well done, thou good and faithful servant: thou hast been faithful over a few things, I will make thee ruler over many things: enter thou into the joy of the lord" (Matthew 25:21).

"Whatever you do, whether it is cleaning toilets or … be the best" (my mother, Mrs. Mildred Hendrickson). "Make sure the work is done well enough that you would put your name on it" (my father, Mr. Harry Hendrickson). 'Know that we are not responsible for what people do to us. We are responsible for our response to what they do' (my epiphany, Dr. Avis Hendrickson).

# *About the Author*

## "Education is the Key ... to Opportunities"

There has to be a better way to live! Early in life, I knew that even without the benefit of experience, exposure, or knowledge, there had to be a better state of existence. As a child, all I knew was a household with a mother, brother, and father, and an extended family of uncles, cousins, and aunts on both maternal and paternal sides, who never came together as one unit—clannish and closed to outsiders. There were also the neighbors in the building, on the block, and other children I spent time with and befriended. That was in the 1960s when this conscientiousness set in. I still remember the moment I heard the news that President Kennedy had been shot. My bearings for national safety were shaken. I listened to understand how the country and my world would recover.

Another memory is of sitting in a junior high school class, silently saying to myself or writing in the margin of my notebook, 'Help me, somebody! Lord, please Help Me!' I lived a sheltered life as a girl in my parents' home. I learned directions from them and the elders in my family, overhearing conversations—children were to be seen and not heard. I learned from school, friends from the neighborhood, and reading books.

That was the era of censored information, even on television. In essence, I knew nothing about the world and relationships beyond my childhood experiences at home. I also realize that at that time in my life, and for some time afterward, my moral character was less informed by Christian standards, as prescribed by the Bible, than it is now. Amen.

I didn't know I was pregnant. While eating hominy grits at breakfast one morning, I left the table, went to the bathroom, and threw up my breakfast. Returning to the kitchen, my mother asked what had happened. I told her. She made a doctor's appointment for me. The results were the beginning of an awakening for me. After the doctor's visit, I later learned that he had advised my mother to put me away in a home for girls. She refused!

Fast-forward through my journey, which has carried me through several years and experiences, I am at a place in my life where I have earned a doctoral degree. The accomplishment occurred while being a married, single parent, caring for four dependent children, and later, the primary caregiver for my mother while advancing in my professional career to become a college administrator. Look at me now!

It was only God who guided my efforts based on my faith. In retrospect, a catalyst for moving fast, meaning deliberate (informed) acceleration on a path forward and upward, was a heightened awareness that I had very little time to live. After giving birth to my first child (while married) at age sixteen, a son, it was then that I learned I had the sickle cell anemia trait. In 1968, the only information I had on the disease was what I overheard in conversations.

There were snippets of information. I heard that in Africa, the disease saved people from malaria. In the United States, it led to death. I didn't know the difference between the disease and the trait. At the age of sixteen, I thought my life would end by the time I was twenty-one. My commitment was to make sure my son would be taken care of similarly to how I would personally invest in his wellbeing. I thought my mother would care for him, and my brother would help. I believed they understood and would support the quality of life I wanted for my son Joseph. Much credit goes to my mother, who made it clear, "You make your bed hard, you lie in it." Therefore, I made plans to manage my responsibility.

Among the vital takeaways from my first marriage is my insistence that all decisions that affect my life must include my input. He, my husband, was in high school training in auto mechanics. We started out our marriage living in my mother's two-bedroom apartment in a tenement building. She worked as a nurse's aide in the evenings. He, the baby, and I slept in my bedroom.

I would sit with my husband in the evenings to help him study so that he could graduate, and he did graduate from high school. My impression was that after he graduated, he would get a job and go to work. One evening, he came home and announced he was enlisting in the Army. No discussion. He had signed up for military service. I thought I would eventually relocate wherever he was stationed. The short version of the story is that it didn't happen.

For a few months, I attended a school for pregnant girls in order to continue my education until the birth of our son. Then I returned to public high school and graduated with an academic diploma on time with my graduating class. There was a high school counselor—male, white, nicknamed the "dirty old man" by the white girls—with whom I spoke about attending college. His response was, "Get a job—become a secretary." I filled out the college application without his input. My first choice was law at John Jay College of Criminal Justice. I was accepted. I wanted to become a lawyer to keep my father and brother out of jail.

Before attending college, and while my husband was in active service overseas, I worked at the telephone company. I would get through the work shifts and split shifts by calculating what I'd be able to purchase with the money I earned. For example, I knew that three hours would enable me to buy my son a pair of shoes, etc.

Apparently, the quality of my work led to my supervisors discussing a promotion for me. This was brought to my attention when I gave notice that I was resigning to attend college. I was offered a supervisory position if I stayed. I resigned.

I learned life through observations and direct experiences. The observations showed me what to do or not do, as a result of the outcomes others experienced from their different interactions and behaviors in various situations. Their life choices informed my life choices. From direct experiences, I learned what I wanted by figuring out what I did not want. Through much of my womanhood, relationships, three additional children, and another marriage, I learned and understood what I wanted through experiences, which clearly spoke to what I did not want in relationships and informed my quality of life.

My exposure was so limited—a sheltered life—that when I was let out, trial and error established my standards for a higher calling. Early in my womanhood—making my own decisions and accepting the responsibility of the consequences—people would say, "You are strong." At that time, "strong" to me meant physical. I knew I wasn't physically strong; mentally, I questioned how they came to that conclusion. Later in life, I understood that they were referring to a standard and the principles under which I operate, which I maintain to the closest degree possible. Seldom did I have to learn things twice. This characteristic may be reflective of my belief and conscious state of the imposed health-related time restraint associated with sickle cell anemia.

Each of my children came with unique circumstances and learning experiences, requiring me to fight emotionally, spiritually, financially, and physically to overcome external threats to my stability, wellness, and sense of self. I desired and worked at maintaining a state of peace and stability and guarding against and eliminating disruptions. This was essential to my perception of maintaining and managing a state of family wellbeing. As my mother said about her care for my brother and me, "We didn't ask to be here." In essence, the children had to be taken care of as best as possible.

My second child, Aaron, was born twelve years after my first child. Within three years after Aaron's birth, my third and youngest son Elijah and daughter Glory were born. I have been honored by my children's existence—Joseph, my first born, Aaron, my birthday gift (born on my birthday), Elijah, my youngest son (babe), and Glory, my precious daughter and sugar dumpling. Our family grew while I simultaneously worked full-time—except for periods of unemployment, childbearing, and help from welfare until I found employment—and attended college to advance the quality of our lives.

Federal and civil rights legislation incorporates the term "no child left behind," and this signifies the plan I implemented and operated for our development. For me, in our household, it was practiced daily. Dr. J. O'Leary is known for the statement, "And how are the children?" My children were and are my constant occupation. It was important to me to maintain the importance of each child's development; no one's development would be sacrificed for that of another. There were times when each child attended the same enrichment program. For example, the community center operated a music school, offering lessons on various instruments, where they all took lessons.

My oldest son learned to swim and worked as a lifeguard during the summer when he first obtained his student working permit. My younger children took swimming lessons. Scheduling the calendar of activities required meticulous attention. Often, I had the assistance of my mother, who would pick them up or be at my home when they arrived from school, if necessary. We made use of after-school programs. During their pre-teens and teen years, we lived in a complex where there was a supervised playground.

Keeping people out of my business was necessary to care for my children. I had to overcome the inference of others. They imposed limitations on my personal sense of the manageability of all my assignments as a mother, student, and employee, including family obligations, societal expectations for maintenance of my home, and relationships.

There were systems that had authority and watch-care over our existence: the schools they attended, medical health care, the church, neighborhood, and family. Any activities brought to their attention, outside of their prescribed general rules for applicable operating processes, would bring an intrusion that would likely distract from my forward momentum to my goal, to give attention and effort to issues that could have been avoided.

Intrusions lurked everywhere. In the context of the social climate in which I lived, the situation of being a first-generation college student meant that access to role models who had the experience and knowledge, or who worked in the systems of authority within environments through which I had to move, were scarce. I lacked pre-knowledge and insight into what is involved in moving through each day in a foreign environment and to personally operate to advance my level in the social, educational, and professional arenas without neglecting my responsibilities.

Therefore, I took another path and existed under different circumstances. Case in point: one day in a casual discussion with my faculty colleague at the college where I had completed my undergraduate work—it was an honor to be hired by my alma mater—she shared her displeasure with the plight of her older son. He was dating a woman who had had a child by another man. She called it "a mess." In silence, I recoiled, knowing that I too was a woman with child(ren), without the Father Knows Best or Dr. Huxtable family images portrayed on television. In effect, if she knew my situation, rather than what I may have appeared to be or what she assumed, she would have considered me a mess as well. It was a derogatory reference that I would not own.

Learning the processes and systems for each industry is the key to advancement. Each system has unwritten rules and written rules; only a relationship with God moved me through these experiences without harm and guided me in providing an appropriate response for circumstances beforehand unknown to me.

Attending school meetings with my children's teachers was important for my children's development. I'm thankful that meetings were held in both the mornings and evenings, providing alternative times to attend. How my children were perceived affected their advancement. I spoke up on a few occasions when the school system attempted to track them out of the prescribed order for their academic progression.

On one occasion, my oldest son's course schedule eliminated the math sequence that would allow him to go to college. I insisted that he be given academic math. My son rose to the occasion. I expected him to learn math, and he did. In another instance, my youngest son, while in elementary school, probably fourth grade, was characterized as not speaking. I strongly suggested that the teacher give him open-ended questions rather than yes-or-no questions that required no other response. I further illustrated to the authorities who were evaluating my child that every morning, religiously, we read a Bible verse and short story, with each child taking turns reading aloud the story on different days and each being required to explain its meaning.

This was before they left for school. Each child also ate breakfast in the mornings. Breakfast was imperative to me. Although I prepared lunches that I considered nutritious for them, I wasn't sure whether they ate during the day outside of the home. I further informed the evaluators that the King James Bible is written on the eighth-grade level. Surely my children could read and have a degree of mastery of comprehension.

Managing the mornings and evenings impacted the quality of my life and the lives of my children. The atmosphere in the home had to be conducive to a healthy existence. The Bible readings and prayer contributed to the establishment of peace in the atmosphere at home.

> *Managing the mornings and evenings impacted the quality of my life and the lives of my children. The atmosphere in the home had to be conducive to a healthy existence.*

About a year into the marriage, we moved from a two-bedroom tenement building to a two-bedroom project apartment. In those days, moving to the projects from the tenement building was considered a step up in social class. My mother, brother, and son moved into the apartment while my husband was in the Army. Later my mother got her own project apartment, and my brother moved in with her. After the birth of my two additional sons and second marriage, we moved to a two-bedroom apartment in a gated co-op community.

It is at the co-op that my children spent most of their developmental years. For many of those years, I was a married, single parent. By social standards, I was out-of-place in the established class of a luxury co-op environment. In my mind, that co-op symbolized our place in the social strata.

I learned through these living experiences that although the door is closed to your apartment, sounds travel. I did not want to give reason to support unsavory ideas of disorder in my living situation. Even with four children, seldom did I raise my voice or allow them to shout in the house unnecessarily. In support of creating a nurturing atmosphere, I would wake them gently with a softly voiced "good morning," often repeating the waking notice. In this way, neither they nor I had our spirits vexed by a loud disruption in the home. I encouraged them to call each other by their name rather than anything even remotely derogatory. I also practiced calling them by their name or an endearing nickname.

From early in their lives, my children understood that they were going to go to college. My preference was for them to go away to college. I saw that experience as essential to their development. They would learn to live outside the home—making constructive use of their time—while I was still available to help them. I had not prepared financially for this desire, yet it was not a deterrent to my insistence that they go to college. I came to learn that God blesses effort based on faith.

To God goes all the glory for the great things He has done directly and through people and circumstances to fulfill His promise to us: "The thief cometh not, but for to steal, and to kill, and to destroy: I am come that they might have life, and that they might have it more abundantly" (John 10:10).

Decades later, having moved through life-changing experiences, I came to realize that there are different levels of advancement, and each level has its own stages and phases. This occurs in all of life's relationships. Consider that a mother remains a mother throughout her life and that of the child. The types of interaction and degrees of responsibility change as the age factor increases. For all relationships, there are frames of reference for operating.

After many years of social engagement and professional advancement, I've established guidelines for operating in different environments:

- Everyone is important—janitor, clerk, secretary, colleague, supervisor, etc.

- Like in a chess game, every piece counts and has a prescribed role. Nevertheless, it is careless for a queen to be captured by a pawn. Stay alert to your environment.

- Excuses do not relieve you of responsibility.

- There are systems and processes in each level of existence. At each level, there is a stratification/characterization. Several dimensions are in operation simultaneously. Access is restricted yet obtainable.

In synopsis, I am a first-generation college graduate who earned her doctorate while caring for her four children. I have authored articles and a short devotional story and given presentations to the community, church, and various civic and educational organizations. My presentations are geared toward allowing audiences to get the best out of themselves and raise their potential effectiveness in personal development.

My career experiences include effectively managing and administering systems and processes, as well as multiple responsibilities across diverse functional areas that impact the lives of people from multiethnic and multicultural backgrounds. I have worked with people with various degrees of preparation, backgrounds, and experiences. My ministry is to connect with people who have a desire to help themselves move forward and advance to the next level.

My career has been as an educator in the higher education arena, serving as a college administrator with a student-affairs background. The primary area of my experience has been providing leadership in collaborations with student, academic, and administrative affairs to increase student enrollment, retention, and completion. I am a knowledgeable collaborator with faculty, staff, students, and external constituencies in managing systems and processes that have an impact on students' abilities to transform their lives in order to reach their fullest potential as members of the greater community.

I have experience in various types of institutions, including community and senior colleges and universities in urban, suburban, rural, and metropolitan communities, as well as public, private, city, state, and religious organizations. My professional background also includes academic affairs, with experience in teaching and expanding the revenue base by initiating contracts with external constituencies for credit and non-credit courses, and obtaining, implementing, and successfully receiving refunding of grants.

My commitment is to help people who want to help themselves reach their fullest potential. In addition to the services managed in the higher education arena, I am the featured speaker and presenter for Educational

# About the Author

Consultation Services. The focus of ECS is to work with people by offering workshops and presentations that provide an understanding of how to reach the fullest potential through the practical application of biblical references and personal development strategies.

The presentations and workshops inspire audiences to overcome challenges and obstacles that may impede their pursuit of success. As an educator, administrator, businesswoman, and family-oriented person, the acquired experiences, knowledge, and God-given wisdom are used to mentor and counsel people who want to make changes to improve the quality of their lives.

Presentations have been made to diverse audiences such as non-profit organizations, private sector businesses, church organizations, and college groups. In my professional career, I have served in leadership positions, including college president of a faith-based institution, vice president at an urban senior college, and president of a national board of directors for a professional organization. My background includes teaching on the college and secondary school levels and serving as a counselor.

***

Dr. Avis Hendrickson has served the Seventh-day Adventist Church in many capacities, both in her home church and sister churches. She has presented workshops for Women's Ministry and Family Life Ministry. Dr. Hendrickson has published articles, including one in the Seventh-day Adventist women's devotional, *In God's Garden* (2000). She has received a wide range of awards and recognition. Her doctorate is in Developmental Education: Student Development and Personnel Services.

Dr. Hendrickson's source for all good gifts is God, through the indwelling of His Holy Spirit, on behalf of the merits of Jesus Christ. Amen. Thank you.

Dr. Hendrickson may be contacted through Educational Consultation Services for speaking engagements, seminars, and training that provide an understanding of how to get to the fullest potential through the practical application of Biblical references and personal development strategies.

Email: drhendrickson@outlook.com

# *Preface*

I hope my story will serve to point readers to the application of biblical principles as the foundation for personal development and professional advancement. There is an old cliché: "I wasn't born with a silver spoon in my mouth."

There are those who have only one thing to do. For them, a reasonable expectation is for that one thing to be done well. I think of young people who graduate from high school and enter college as resident students. Those students only have to go to class, study, sleep, and eat at the cafeteria at an institution providing room, board, and education. Those persons should become scholars. Yet, some in this position succumb to activities that distract them from their purpose for attending the institution.

In contrast, a person may have no academic obligations, but merely a J.O.B.—what I tend to call Just-Over-Broke. The job is characterized as having no upward mobility. That person should work in such a way that leads to a new position, with position having upward mobility. Become a company person or a worker with a career.

Neither of the above situations was my path, and under disadvantaged circumstances I achieved levels of higher education and professional advancement. Some of the lessons I learned are as follows:

Before completing high school, I was married and the mother of a baby son. I went from a sheltered childhood to an existence in which I was naïve. My guidepost through my naiveté was remembering my mother saying, "Education is the key." In the culture of my childhood, under my parents' roof, when they spoke, it was as though God had spoken. A child did not talk back or ask questions. In fact, it was an era when a child was seen and not heard. I wanted to know, "Key to what?" I never asked.

It was as an adult that I realized, 'Education is the key to opportunities to improve the quality of life for myself, my family, and the community.' At this writing, I have four children, a doctoral degree, and over the tenure of my career, I have professionally advanced through the college-level ranks, including counselor, faculty, dean, vice president, and college president, as well as a board-of-trustees member.

"Because he hath set his love upon me, therefore will I deliver him: I will set him on high, because he hath known my name" (Ps. 91:14). I thank God for guiding me through these different life experiences, keeping me from harm and ensnarement, molding my development in each phase of this life-changing journey.

My background prepares me to advance in higher realms of service.

> Then Mordecai commanded to answer Esther, Think not with thyself that thou shalt escape in the king's house, more than all the Jews. For if thou altogether holdest thy peace at this time, *then* shall there enlargement and deliverance arise to the Jews from another place; but thou and thy father's house shall be destroyed: and who knoweth whether thou are come to the kingdom for *such* a time as this? (Esther 4:13, 14)

# *Introduction*

    Lifestyle and personal development constitute a lifelong process of guided activities that lead to reaching your fullest potential, all while operating in the realm of a state of wellness. The intent of this written work is to provide an understanding of how to get to your fullest potential through the practical application of biblical references and personal development strategies. You'll never become who you want to be by remaining who you are.

    Breakthroughs forward on your life's path to the next level are new experiences. At first, the new place is unfamiliar for a short period of time, and the guideposts are not immediately evident. You will have to feel your way forward in a state of confidence. Biblically, confidence is understood to be faith. I have come to realize that faith is an exercise in patience. The new place will seem spacious and unfamiliar.

    In the midst of the unknown, refer to the source of all resources—the Bible. Think of B.I.B.L.E. as an acronym for **B**asic **I**nstructions **B**efore **L**eaving **E**arth. Scripture will be the basis for the principles of a state of wellness. At times like these, your footing should be on a sure foundation, the B.I.B.L.E. "For bodily exercise profiteth little: but godliness is profitable unto all things, having promise of the life that now is, and of that which is to come" (1 Tim. 4:8).

## *A New Perspective on Life*

Do you feel that there has to be a better way? There is! Do you want to move out of the present place of struggling or surviving to the place of living and thriving? There is guidance in the Scriptures on how to move forward: "Thus saith the Lord, thy Redeemer, the Holy One of Israel: I am the Lord thy God which teacheth thee to profit, which leadeth thee by the way that thou shouldest go" (Isa. 48:17).

Life happens. Some people say, "Stuff happens" (that's the clean version). The nature of life is for things to happen. The determining factor on how situations will affect you is your reaction and response to them. We only control our reactions to what occurs. Some situations press on us as though to threaten our balance and sense of self. Some arise and appear to be greater than we can handle. Others can strike fear in us. On these occasions, take a moment to realize that every situation that arises in life becomes manageable when you are determined not to be afraid and think through what should be done to get through the situation.

> *The determining factor on how situations will affect you is your reaction and response to them.*

For those times when you feel unable to think, call on the name of Jesus to give you clarity. It is always helpful to plan your work and work your plan, making adjustments according to God's guidance. The one factor that puts things into perspective and makes them all manageable is knowing "who you are and whose you are" (Lowery).

Scripture says that God would not allow any temptation that you cannot overcome. "There hath no temptation taken you but such as is common to man: but God is faithful, who will not suffer you to be tempted above that ye are able; but will with the temptation also make a way to escape, that ye may be able to bear it" (1 Cor. 10:13).

Also, nothing separates me from the love of God. "Nay, in all these things we are more than conquerors through him that loves us. For I am persuaded, that neither death, nor life, nor angels, nor principalities, nor powers, nor things present, nor things to come, Nor height, nor depth, nor any other creature, shall be able to separate us from the love of God, which is in Christ Jesus our Lord" (Rom. 8:37–39).

The key is to know that you can only overcome through reliance on the strength of God, through Jesus Christ, with the guidance of His Holy Spirit. With this perspective, you can say, "Thank you, God, for trusting me to rely on You to overcome every situation that attempts to rob me of the joy of a close relationship with God through Christ Jesus. Thank you for having the confidence in me to praise You always." "Trust in the Lord with all thine heart; and lean not unto thine own understanding" (Prov. 3:5).

You have lived long enough to see evidence in your life that God, through Jesus Christ, has shown you favor in other matters in the past. "Finally, brethren, whatsoever things are true, whatsoever things are honest, whatsoever things are just, whatsoever things are pure, whatsoever things are lovely, whatsoever things are of good report; if there be any virtue, and if there be any praise, think on these things" (Phil. 4:8). Remember Job's loyalty to God, even when he lost everything! "Though he slay me, yet will I trust in him: but I will maintain mine own ways before him" (13:15).

Optimally, the process of reaching your fullest potential will incorporate principles of operating in a state of wellness, regardless of your station in life. Wellness is your state of health—spiritually, emotionally, intellectually, physically, socially, financially, and sexually. Your health in these areas is determined by your state of affairs, not necessarily by having to give each area equal percentages of your life resources.

Getting refreshed has its place in this state of wellness. "Refreshed"—"to restore the strength and vigor of a person" (*Oxford American Dictionary*, 1980). There is a relationship between "refreshed" and "rest." The act of rest is embedded in the concept of refreshment. Everything made comes with the manufacturer's instructions. With God as our creator, make the Bible your source of instructions. God rested. "And on the seventh day God ended his work which he had made; and he rested on the seventh day from all his work which he had made" (Gen. 2:2).

Jesus had time alone—retirement from His public ministry. "And he said unto them, Come ye yourselves apart into a desert place, and rest a while: for there were many coming and going, and they had no leisure so much as to eat" (Mark 6:31).

Being harassed, harried, rushed, and busy are not signs of righteousness. Refer to Martha:

> Now it came to pass, as they went, that he entered into a certain village: and a certain woman named Martha received him into her house. And she had a sister called Mary, which also sat at Jesus' feet, and heard his word. But Martha was cumbered about much serving, and came to him, and said, Lord dost thou not care that my sister hath left me to serve alone? bid her therefore that she help me. And Jesus answered and said unto her, Martha, Martha, thou art careful and troubled about many things: But one thing is needful: and Mary hath chosen that good part, which shall not be taken away from her. (Luke 10:38–42)

A refreshing is embedded in the Sabbath. "Wherefore the children of Israel shall keep the sabbath, to observe the sabbath throughout their generations, for a perpetual covenant. It is a sign between me and the children of Israel for ever: for in six days the Lord made heaven and earth, and on the seventh day he rested, and was refreshed" (Ex. 31:16, 17). "And [Jesus] said unto them, The sabbath was made for man, and not man for the sabbath" (Mark 2:27).

## Every Day You Make Choices: Define the Basis for Your Choice

### *A New Perspective on Your Mission in Relationship to God and Others*

Your mission starts with self and permeates your surroundings—home, family, community. The great commission is found in Matthew 28:18–20. Emphasis should be given to verse 20: "Teaching them to observe all things whatsoever I have commanded you: and, lo, I am with you alway, even unto the end of the world. Amen." This mission is an assignment for every disciple of Jesus, regardless of age, social class, economics, education, etc. For the purpose of this writing, a disciple is one who accepts and helps spread the teachings of Jesus.

> *The best example of how to fulfill this mission is Jesus, who used every opportunity presented to Him to do good for the benefit of others. He always pointed people to the heavenly Father.*

The best example of how to fulfill this mission is Jesus, who used every opportunity presented to Him to do good for the benefit of others. He always pointed people to the heavenly Father. "The Spirit of the Lord is upon me, because he hath anointed me to preach the gospel to the poor; he hath sent me to heal the brokenhearted, to preach deliverance to the captives, and recovering of sight to the blind, to set at liberty them that are bruised, To preach the acceptable year of the Lord" (Luke 4:18, 19).

The following are examples of practical and manageable ways to share the good news in every aspect of your life. Starting with yourself, each morning that you are blessed to wake up, let your first conversation be with God in prayer. In your prayers, include expressions of thankfulness, supplication, etc. Then engage in Scripture reading and devotional time.

In your home, create an atmosphere where Jesus would like to dwell. In conversation, behavior, and engagement with others, exhibit a kindness that only the indwelling of God's Holy Spirit would make possible.

With immediate and extended family members, share stories of God's favor to you, as witnessed in your daily activities through struggle, surviving, and living. These snapshots of life's experiences direct people to God, His mercy, and lovingkindness. Yes, even coming from you, telling people who know of your acts of ungodliness will point them to your change in character through God's grace. The act of being born again furthers your ability to work in your mission field. Be encouraged in your discipleship, "For God hath not given us the spirit of fear; but of power, and of love, and of a sound mind" (2 Tim. 1:7).

Community is an extension of where you live. Extend invitations to people in your community to attend church, Bible studies, and prayer meetings. Understand that an invitation is not an obligation to attend.

You can start working on your mission now, with a smile. Smiling is a universal language that breaks through all barriers. Also, when you speak, offer an encouraging word as you move through the community, whether you know the person or not. May God be with you always as you fulfill your mission. Withholding kindness is like a dead sea—nothing grows. You become stagnant and stink, needing movement, so that God's goodness flows through you.

Decision-making is a great responsibility. This occurs all the time, whether we take action or decide to do nothing. Which action or inaction you take has outcomes that determine the quality of your life. Consider where your daily activities are taking you. If life is a journey, like a train ride, there is a map to use as a guide to determine which path to take. To get to a given destination, no matter what type of transportation, you need a map or instruction on how to get from where you are to where you want to go. Your responsibility is to become familiar with the information: where to find it, how to read it, what to look for, why it applies to you, and when to utilize it.

The "why" for having the travel information is to plan how you will arrive at your desired location. Even with all the information, you must take action if you want your lifestyle to change. Doing the same thing and expecting something to change is defined as insanity (Albert Einstein).

When you are ready to move forward in the direction that improves your lifestyle, at the center of that change is your personal development. The following material is intended to provoke the reader to engage in self-directed learning, drawing the answers by applying the information. Movement forward activates a process that will take you outside of your comfort zone and into a space of actualizing possibilities.

Moving forward to the next step is doable. "I can do all things through Christ which strengtheneth me" (Phil. 4:13). There is a process to follow to accomplish the goal of moving forward, and the steps should be taken in the prescribed sequence.

Working with three components and several elements in each will move you forward to your next level. The process can be repeated as often as you want to move forward. The components are vision, mission, and measurable actions.

Starting this process requires having a definition for each term. The definitions should serve to guide and inform your structured process. In the book *The Richest Man Who Ever Lived* by Steven Scott, vision is defined as "a clearly defined dream, idea, goal, or objective and a plan detailing the specific steps that must be taken to achieve it" (2006, p. 33).

Mission is a commitment to a standard (of operating) by which you are going to live and apply to all that you do. In the book *Repositioning*

*Yourself*, T. D. Jakes refers to creating a "Personal Mission Statement, who you are and what you're about. This identifies your personal brand; what you consistently contribute by your presence and gifting" (2007, p. 15). To further clarify, mission is defined as acting in ways that are consistent across the broad spectrum of private and public behaviors.

The measurable actions component has several elements:

1. An orderly process

2. Identifying goals

3. Dividing goal(s) into step-by-step objectives that collectively and progressively lead to accomplishing the goal(s)

4. Setting a timeline and developing a manageable plan for achieving each objective

The title of a book by Bill Hogan illustrates the process of reaching your goal: *How Do You Eat an Elephant? One Bite at a Time!*

## Change Is Interesting. Who Takes Responsibility for It?

Every action has consequences. When you attribute what you've done to "The devil made me do it," that is not an excuse that will relieve you of the responsibility of your actions. Years ago, there was a show on television, and the main character, Flip Wilson, would say the above quote in almost every episode. That phrase would always draw laughter from the audience and be used after he was caught in some wrongdoing. He never admitted responsibility for his behavior. Someone else was always responsible. What made it more pronounced was that in this series, Flip Wilson was a mature, older man. That is television.

We definitely reap the consequences of our behavior. In this world, wrongdoings have serious repercussions. Through an act of God, we can recover from the harm of a pattern of destructive behavior. The choices we make are driven by our understanding.

Every profession has literature that informs and guides the practice, such as grammar texts and books of instruction in teaching. The products we use also come with instructions, whether it's an iron, furniture that needs to be assembled, etc. Life has a book of instructions as well: the Bible.

When you know what's going on around you, your response to the situation, in most cases, will be in your best interest. That is the natural instinct of responding. Few are interested in knowingly harming themselves when it can be avoided. Those who would intentionally harm themselves are dangerous people. They are also likely to harm others.

Understanding your situation will inform your response. The actions you take can be traced and are connected through the rules and prescribed standards for the system in which you are oriented.

For any product, the best instructions for its operation are those provided by the manufacturer. Consider God as your Maker and the Bible your instructions manual. Given that the benefit of understanding drives your choices, the Bible speaks to framing what it means. "Give instruction to a wise man, and he will be yet wiser: teach a just man, and he will increase in learning. The fear of the Lord is the beginning of wisdom: and the knowledge of the holy is understanding" (Prov. 9:9, 10). "And unto man he said, Behold, the fear of the Lord, that *is* wisdom; and to depart from evil *is* understanding" (Job 28:28).

Consider the word "fear." In the above verses, "fear" refers to honoring, obeying, and the like. According to *Unger's Bible Dictionary*, "It is produced in the soul by the Holy Spirit and great blessing is pronounced upon those who possess this Christian trait ... It dreads God's displeasure, desires his favor, reveres his holiness, submits cheerfully to his will, is grateful for his benefits, sincerely worships him, and conscientiously obeys his commandments" (Unger 1983, p. 348).

Choices are within your realm of authority. Even when you delegate the authority over your life to someone else, you are still responsible for your actions. Relinquishing authority does not exonerate you from the responsibility. The power to withstand encroachments into your sense of self is within your right to choose. "Submit yourselves therefore to God. Resist the devil, and he will flee from you" (James 4:7).

You can choose to re-attain previously relinquished authority over your choices. Here's how: Decide on the standard under which you will operate. Our Creator gave the following instructions:

> Only be thou strong and very courageous, that thou mayest observe to do according to all the law, which Moses my servant commanded thee: turn not from it *to* the right hand or *to* the left, that thou mayest prosper whithersoever thou goest. This book of the law shall not depart out of thy mouth; but thou shalt meditate therein day and night, that thou mayest observe to do according to all that is written therein: for then thou shalt make thy way prosperous, and then thou shalt have good success. (Joshua 1:7, 8)

> *When you arrive at the place in your sense of self where you realize that there must be a better way, you're ready to invest in the change process. You may stumble around in your search for a better way, or you may choose the tried and true way—the Bible.*

When you arrive at the place in your sense of self where you realize that there must be a better way, you're ready to invest in the change process. You may stumble around in your search for a better way, or you may choose the tried and true way—the Bible.

## Framing Your Advancement

"Success is to be measured not so much by the position that one has reached in life as by the obstacles which he has overcome while trying to succeed" (Washington). Success is defined by the individual. The key to what influences your judgment is words—words you hear, read, and say.

"The words we use react on our thoughts and have the power to affect the character" (Douglass 2015, p. 191). Words are powerful. They are at the beginning of all activity. "And God said … and it was so" (Gen. 1:3, 7, 9, etc.).

Jesus is the pattern and example by which to measure your choices and decisions. He overcame at His weakest point in humanity when He was tempted in the wilderness after fasting forty days and nights. His foremost weapon was, "It is Written" (Matt. 4:4, 7, 10).

Sticks and stone will break your bones, and words will harm or heal you. Words are powerful and may affect your sense of wellness. "Death and life *are* in the power of the tongue: and they that love it shall eat the fruit thereof" (Prov. 18:21). "It is the spirit that quickeneth; the flesh profiteth nothing: the words that I speak unto you, they are spirit, and they are life" (John 6:63).

I gleaned the following from a TV presentation by Dr. Creflo Dollar, pastor of World Changers Church International:

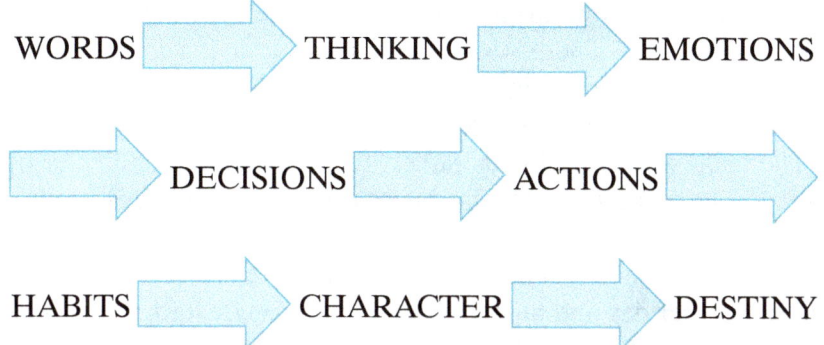

Words: The Word of God and confidence therein.

Thinking: Who's framing the way you think? Change your thinking, change your life.

Emotions: Controlling your emotions determines whether you experience a blessing or a curse. Blessings line up with the Word of God.

Decisions: Making informed judgments

Actions: What you do will determine the manifestation (actions cause the increase to take place).

Habits: These line up with the Word of God.

Character: Doing what's right, in the right way, because it's right. We cultivate character with every choice we make in life.

Destiny: Where you will end up, or with what you will end up.

## A Perspective on Your Value

Men and women, including you and me, are an expression of God's love. The beginning of my story, as far back as I can remember, captures snapshots of time that I can still recall—snapshots of life-impacting events. With hindsight, I'm able to connect them as being foundational to my spiritual, emotional, intellectual, physical, social, financial, and sexual nature.

It all comes together for me through this framing story. Whether I read it or heard it, I'm not sure, but it has stayed with me from childhood. It's a version of a knight-in-shining-armor type of story. The setting is in Arabia, or some other seemingly exotic, distant place where life was much different than my experience was (as I remembered it at the tender age of about seven; I'm not sure of my age at the time the story made an impression on me). There was a young boy. He had a mentor who was responsible for his education, training, social development, and growth into manhood as his inherited role was to become king of a vast nation.

The child was loved by his father, the current king and ruler of his universe. The mentor lived in the palace with the king and his family. The child's development was monitored by his parents and the elders in the royal court. The mentor and the boy had a very close relationship, as he was his overseer day and night. With the boy's kingly status, he was never beaten for wrongdoing. Instead, his mentor suffered the painful consequences. As their relationship grew, it was the closeness between them that ultimately gave the future king reason to pay attention to the suffering the mentor had endured on his behalf.

Gradually, the boy king's defiance of instructions and intentional disobedience lessened as he saw the results of the pain his caregiver and longtime friend and companion had endured for him. Despite his bad behavior, the mentor still loved him and continued to train and teach him. As the king continued to review his son's development, he was pleased with the degree of excellence he portrayed. He was confident that the boy king would develop to display divine excellence as a representative of the throne. This story may speak to our relationship with Jesus.

As I grew older, I was able to put into context "consequences for behavior." Yes, the proverbial "don't touch the stove because it's hot; only to touch the stove to get burned" applies. When you are in a group with the syndrome of "crabs in a barrel," doing what the other crabs do, you're limited to keeping the status quo. When one crab makes an effort to climb out and do life differently, the others pull on its feet to bring it back into place or bite to disable the crab from escaping the barrel.

However, with persistence, there are crabs who get out of the barrel—the proverbial glass ceiling. The crabs that attempt to climb out are moving toward the light—a light with rays that gleam through the narrow slats in the wooden cover of the barrel. No other promises exist in the bottom of the crab-infested barrel environment. All hope exists in moving toward the light. There must be a better way. This is what I interpose as the silent motivating drive to move differently and sometimes alone. There must be a better way of living.

Another statement that encapsulates the intent of the message is something Pastor Wintley Phipps said, "People feed pigeons, but they shoot at eagles." Here's another bird story. An eagle left the nest of her eggs to get food. Upon her takeoff, one egg fell out of the nest and landed in the patch of grass where chickens were feeding. The hen standing nearby on the ground embraced the egg and sat on it until it hatched.

That eaglet only knew its immediate surroundings. It acclimated to cackling and eating food like a chicken. As time passed, the baby eagle mimicked the little chicks—walking with its head down, plucking food from the ground, etc. It and the other chicks noticed a difference in the growth of the eagle grafted in as a chicken. As it grew, it acknowledged that it did not look like the chickens. It had a sense of being different.

Day after day, they just kept up their routine. One day, as they moved about the farm in the sunlight, the eagle noticed a shadow on the ground of a flying object from above. As the other chickens looked in fright, the eagle looked in reflection. It caught a glimpse of itself. The eaglet had wings that were longer than those of its companion chickens, which had not been exercised to their full expansion, and the beak of the little eagle looked similar to the flying bird.

The eaglet stretched its wings like the flying bird it watched above. It pondered and knew it didn't belong with the cackling chickens and purposed to fly like the eagle. Eventually, through practice and disregard for the chickens' cackling comments and expectations, it began to fly. The eaglet had decided to fly and not be on the ground with the chickens.

To have a purpose is to be intentional like the eagle in moving through atmospheres and environments. Our purpose is to be of service to God in whatever station we may be, through our daily activities and interactions with and influence on others. I've heard it said that people are in our lives for a reason, season, or lifetime. This suggests to me that life is fluid, in motion, and changing.

Eagles are a national treasure and symbol for the United States. A biblical reference for the eagle is Isaiah 40:31: "But they that wait upon the Lord shall renew *their* strength; they shall mount up with wings as eagles; they shall run, and not be weary; *and* they shall walk, and not faint." I like the following commentary regarding this verse:

> **Wait upon the Lord.** That is, look to the Lord in sincerity and humility for wisdom and strength, and then patiently await His guidance (see on ch. 30:21; cf. 57:15).
>
> **Renew their strength.** The Christian life is a constant process of receiving from God and giving to God. Strength is expended in the service for the Master (cf. Mark 5:30), but there are always new supplies of grace and vitality available from Him who knows not weariness. He who does not continue to receive strength from God will soon find himself in a position where he is unable to serve God. ...
>
> ... **As eagles.** One of the most magnificent sights in the wild is an eagle soaring in the sky, higher and higher, with seemingly little effort. Similarly, the child of God who draws his strength from above is enabled to go ever onward and upward, always reaching new heights of achievement (see Ps. 103:5). Day after day it is the privilege of the Christian to go on from grace to grace and from victory to victory ... Strength is added to strength, and progress is constant. Higher and still higher goals come into view, and eventually the Christian attains to "the prize of the high calling of God in Christ Jesus" (Phil. 3:14). (Nichol, ed., *The Seventh-day Adventist Bible Commentary*, vol. 4, p. 248)

## *Personal Development*

Many, many times, I've moved through environments where others imposed an expectation that I remain the same and within their reach and boundaries of existence—an act of stagnating my development because of their fears. My internal response was, 'Don't measure me by your limitations.' Sometimes, I would encounter hostility to different degrees. My atmosphere was permeated by people's "You think you're better than us" perception. My response (mostly internally in my mind) was, 'Not at all! I'm better than these circumstances and exercising my God-given right to make different choices.'

This right of choice is also embedded in a contemporary, African-American tradition, Kwanzaa. As a young adult, I became aware of Kwanzaa with its seven principles:

1) *Umoja*—unity
2) *Kujichagulia*—self-determination
3) *Ujima*—collective work and responsibility
4) *Ujamaa*—cooperative economics
5) *Nia*—purpose
6) *Kuumba*—creativity
7) *Imani*—faith

*Kujichagulia*, the second of the seven principles, is aligned with the personal right to make choices.

Know that each person is wondrously and marvelously made. ***"I will praise thee; for I am fearfully*** **and** ***wonderfully made: marvellous*** **are** ***thy works: and*** **that** ***my soul knoweth right well"*** (Ps. 139:14). You're allowed to be different. No two snowflakes or other life forms created by God is monotonous in design. A person is robed in his or her beauty when stifled from being unique.

In each movement forward, there were lessons learned—some by experience, some by observation, some immediately, some only by reflective thought. I've encapsulated these lessons into a context of what it takes to be well. Being well is a state of health in your existence. For the purpose of my lessons learned, a state of being is composed of seven elements: spiritual, emotional, intellectual, physical, social, financial, and sexual. Each of these areas of being is significant, indispensable, and connected. The degree of attention to each element is dependent on the need of your state of wellness at any given time.

In a particular article, several counselors offered their definitions of wellness. Excerpts from that article are as follows:

> **Charles V. Lindsey:** ... It means being more aware of the interrelationship between what we think and what we feel and of how our care, or lack of care, for our bodies affects the way we think and how we behave. ...
>
> **Katlin Hecox:** There are many great ways to maintain mind-body wellness. What makes sense to one individual will be different from another client. The first thing is to make sure that clients understand that their thoughts and actions will impact their state of wellness. ...
>
> **Stuart Bonnington:** ... Wellness to me comes down to what are you doing to take care of and nurture yourself in bodymind [sic] and spirit? ...
>
> **Geri Miller:** ... What is it that keeps your spirit alive? I encourage clients to think of themselves as vessels; what are they putting into themselves? (Jenny Christenson, "Making the Mind-Body Connection," *Counseling Today*, February 2009, pages 24-29..

Wellness, with its aforementioned seven elements, for the purpose of this writing, is a prosperous measure of health in every aspect of your life. If you do the same thing, you should not expect anything to change. There is growth in change. "I press toward the mark for the prize of the high calling of God in Christ Jesus" (Phil. 3:14).

The areas of wellness are not equal in their need for attention, but they are equally important. Strength in the spiritual element is referenced in John 3:6, 14:16, 26, and 27. This element pertains to the part related to worship and divine communication. To be filled with the Holy Spirit is to have a mind that is in Christ Jesus.

For the purpose of this writing, there is a distinction between the terms "spiritual" and "religious." The former is about a relationship between the individual and the Creator of the universe. Through God's love, we enter into that relationship by the sacrifice of Jesus Christ. "For God so loved the world, that he gave his only begotten Son, that whosoever believeth in him should not perish, but have everlasting life. For God sent not his Son into the world to condemn the world; but that the world through him might be saved" (John 3:16, 17). In that spiritual relationship, there is a daily indwelling of God's Holy Spirit.

The following insights served to be foundational to my personal development and professional advancement. Spirituality entered my consciousness early in my life through my mother and father. Daddy introduced saying "Grace" at the dinner table. Mommy introduced praying before bedtime.

Kneeling at the bedside, I recited, "Now I lay me down to sleep, I pray the Lord my soul to keep, If I die before I wake, I pray the Lord my soul to take. God bless mommy, daddy, my brother, my aunts, my uncles, my cousins (everyone I could think of by name). Amen." I was satisfied, for I knew nothing else.

Attending church regularly occurred when my mother located one in the neighborhood and felt comfortable with allowing me to walk the few blocks to attend a nondenominational Christian service on Sundays. The Open Door Christian Church was a storefront. Early on in this experience, I started piano lessons. At times, I played the piano during the Sunday services.

We changed churches around the time I reached puberty, when we moved out of the neighborhood. My father intentionally did not pay the rent for our apartment on Third Avenue in the Bronx, and our belongings were put out on the street, evicted, on a school day, while I was attending elementary school. I remember that day. Out of the ordinary, my mother picked me up from school early in the afternoon. Usually, I walked home with the other children. As we walked closer to the tenement building, I noticed furniture and other items out on the curb of the street. As we walked closer, I realized it was from my family's apartment. My mother signaled to me to pick up what I wanted and could carry. We then left.

We moved in with my uncle (mother's brother) and his family. It was a three-bedroom apartment in the projects in the Bronx. I continued school, traveling by bus back and forth. In a short time, my mother moved my brother and me to an apartment in a community different from the previous community in which I lived during my early childhood, different from my uncle's neighborhood. In this Bronx neighborhood, she connected our family with Gethsemane Baptist Church. There, religious activities expanded to baptism and service in auxiliary church organizations. My first marriage took place in that church. My sons were christened in that church. Those religious beginnings wove through all my life. Eventually, all my children and grandchildren were presented for baby blessing and dedication as infants.

For years, between my time at the Baptist and then Adventist church, I had extensive, life-changing experiences and relationships. In my early adulthood, I stopped attending church religiously. Prayer continued in my household, as I had been taught, both at home and through my early religious exposure. This includes the spiritual connection through the Baptist church's gospel music. The message in the music spoke to my core and resonated in my being. Before the break in attending church, I sang in a few choirs. At one point, I served as a secretary to the choir.

Through our mother-daughter relationship, I was introduced to the Seventh-day Adventist Church denomination. From the time I left her house, we continued close contact. I talked with my mother by phone or in person every day. In the summer of 1983, it suddenly became evident that her pattern of behavior had changed. She had to leave every day at 6 p.m. I wanted to know where she was going. It seemed inappropriate to me for her to have a boyfriend she had to meet. I thought, *'Why else would she so determinedly need to end telephone conversations with me in time to leave for her (almost) daily meetings?'*

She declared she was going to church. I asked for the location so that I could attend with her. I wanted to make sure she was in good company. I attended. It was called a tent meeting and held on a lot in the Bronx, near Claremont Parkway. The group was different from the church we attended. I visited the summer tent meetings and found that their sermons were backed by Scripture. Each sermon referred to several passages, which the audience was encouraged to read as part of the church service. "For precept must be upon precept, precept upon precept; line upon line, line upon line; here a little, and there a little" (Isa. 28:10).

I became interested. This happened when I was pregnant with my fourth child, my daughter. After she was born, I was baptized into the Seventh-day Adventist Church. My children and I attended religiously. On occasion, my husband would attend services. I listened, read, studied, learned, and internalized Scriptures. I prayed fervently and developed a personal relationship with an understanding of God's love for me and the world. I actualized the meaning of the B.I.B.L.E. as an acronym: **B**asic **I**nstructions **B**efore **L**eaving **E**arth. There's a treasure of life-enriching guidance in the Bible.

## The First Element of Wellness Is Spiritual

Spiritual epiphanies arose in my consciousness. I began to take ownership of my relationship with God. Prayer became a constant throughout my days, as I walked, drove, talked, worked, and contemplated responsibilities and every other aspect of my life. "Pray without ceasing" (1 Thess. 5:17). In essence, a believer should remain in the attitude of prayer, though not always praying audibly. This mode provides wonderful relief under all circumstances, every time.

All relationships require communication. Prayer is a conversation with God. It needs to be a two-sided communication, for listening is also necesary. I found that God communicates directly through His Word (the Bible), others who the Holy Spirit convicts you as being an affirmation, personal impressions, or circumstances that speak to your situation and are aligned with His standards; as I continue to understand His standards.

> *All relationships require communication. Prayer is a conversation with God. It needs to be a two-sided communication, for listening is also necessary*

In some cultures, a man's word is his bond. In life, the concept of a man's word being his bond is a temporal state of affairs. God's Word is eternal. "Sanctify them through thy truth: thy word is truth" (John 17:17). Here, truth means without error, accurate, reliable, and authoritative.

Scripture has become the language of my prayers. A Bible verse I use in prayer is Isaiah 41:13: "For I the Lord thy God will hold thy right hand, saying unto thee, Fear not; I will help thee." I acknowledge I need help, ask God for it, and receive it openly.

I also believe Matthew 7:7–8 and 11, as well as Psalm 84:11: "Ask, and it shall be given you; seek, and ye shall find; knock, and it shall be opened unto you: For every one that asketh receiveth; and he that seeketh findeth; and to him that knocketh it shall be opened. … If ye then, being evil, know how to give good gifts unto your children, how much more shall your Father which is in heaven give good things to them that ask him?" ("evil" here refers to mankind's sinful nature). "For the Lord God is a sun and shield: the Lord will give grace and glory: no good thing will he withhold from them that walk uprightly."

Over time, I've come to have confidence (meaning faith) in God. There is evidence in my life that He blesses efforts based on faith. I also understand that patience is an exercise in faith.

I once heard that if you want to hide something from a man, put it in writing. The information for an abundant life was there in the Bible the whole time. "The thief cometh not, but for to steal, and to kill, and to destroy: I am come that they might have life, and that they might have it more abundantly" (John 10:10).

Oswald Chambers made a capstone statement on the spiritual experience: "A private relationship of worshiping God is the greatest essential element of spiritual fitness" *(My Utmost for His Highest*, September 10).

I have served the Seventh-day Adventist Church in many capacities, including Sabbath School superintendent, personal ministries band leader, deaconess, family life coordinator, and elder at the Hunts Point Seventh-day Adventist Church in the Bronx. I also worked with the Women's Ministries in the Northeastern Conference and am the seventeenth president to serve Atlantic Union College (AUC) in its 132-year history. AUC is a Seventh-day Adventist institution solely funded by the Atlantic Union Conference (2011–2018).

> That which will bless humanity is spiritual life. If the man is in harmony with God, he will depend continually upon him for strength. "Be ye therefore perfect, even as your Father which is in Heaven is perfect." It should be our life-work to press forward continually toward the perfection of Christian character, ever striving for conformity to the will of God, remembering that the efforts begun upon earth will continue throughout eternity. God has set before

the human family an elevated standard, and he who is true to his God-given manhood, will not only promote the happiness of his fellow-creatures in this life, but will aid them to secure an eternal reward in the life to come. (White, *Reflecting Christ*, p. 157).

All social interactions involve people characterized by varying degrees of commitment, learning, and expectations to the task that they have in common. People are different at different times. The difference in their response is more in their thinking.

Ephesians 6:12. For we wrestle not against flesh and blood, but against principalities, against powers, against the rulers of the darkness of this world, against spiritual wickedness in high places.

Therefore, people change their allegiance dependent on their interests at the time of the encounter. They are not of the same opinion in each situation. A true measure of a person is their response in a crisis.

On my first cruise, standing on the balcony of my stateroom, I looked out at the ocean. As far as I could see, all around the ship was water. In the distance, it looked as though the sea touched the sky. I thought, 'The explorers must have had a profound sense of life that allowed them to travel uncharted seas without any landmark bearings.' If they believed the world was flat, looking out at the vast opening, they surely had reason to think that they would get to the end and fall off the edge. In sharp contrast to that thought pattern, in my elementary and high school history classes, I learned that they did not fall off the globe. In fact, some lived to tell their stories. Perhaps they followed an inner core belief.

While moving forward, others may be walking on the path with you. However, they may only go for a particular distance. Everyone cannot share the unique circumstances that influence their development. Each person is the sum total of their experiences. Everyone can't go where you are going.

The spiritual element refers to being filled with the Holy Spirit, having a mind that is in Christ Jesus. "That which will bless humanity is spiritual life. If the man is in harmony with God, he will depend continually upon Him for strength."

"*He that is* slow to anger *is* better than the mighty; and he that ruleth his spirit than he that taketh a city" (Prov. 16:32).

"It is the spirit that quickeneth; the flesh profiteth nothing: the words that I speak unto you, they are spirit, and they are life" (John 6:63).

"This I say then, Walk in the Spirit, and ye shall not fulfil the lust of the flesh" (Gal. 5:16).

## The Second Element of Wellness Is Emotional

A biblical reference to the emotional element is John 11:35: "Jesus wept." "In His humanity Jesus was touched with human sorrow, and wept with the sorrowing" (Nichol 1980, p. 1015). The word "emotionally" pertains to "receiving impressions through outside stimuli; intense feeling (i.e., love, hate, joy, fear, sorrow, etc.) with accompanying physical movements (*Webster's New Universal Dictionary of the English Language*, Business Encyclopedia Edition, 1972).

> *Emotions are inward reactions that also manifest themselves externally. They are generally based on external stimuli motivated by our perceptions.*

Emotion is to be moved with feelings—an affective state of consciousness—pain, pleasure, disgrace, joy, sorrow, fear, hate, and the like are experienced. Emotions are inward reactions that also manifest themselves externally. They are generally based on external stimuli motivated by our perceptions. These sensations range from one end of the spectrum of reactions, barely affected, to the other end of the spectrum with a response that is out of control.

For example, using either a fly swatter or shotgun on a fly that bugs you (pun intended) is an illustration of a spectrum, considering the range from an appropriate response (fly swatter) to an out-of-control response (shotgun). It's the equivalent of a permanent solution for a short-term problem. An emotional state regarding a temporary situation has long-term, life-impacting results. There is a range of remedies to avert emotional explosions as a response.

We experience several different relationships throughout our lives. In an earlier phase of my relational development, I was lost in my sense of "self" when my "beloved" made it evident that I thought more of my position in the relationship than his actions supported. My perception of his treatment toward me was incongruent with the value I placed on myself and my understanding of the standards in an intimate, committed relationship between a man and woman. My reality of the situation was shattering to my sense of worth and a basis for behavior that created a platform for me to explore and ultimately grow in the clarity of the standards of living in a state of God's peace.

The Lord sustained me through those periods of recovery. I remember, on one occasion, just going through the motions of fulfilling my responsibilities: children had to eat, their clothes needed to be clean, they had to get to school on time, I had to continue to work and bring in a salary, etc. My image of myself was diminished. The beauty was absent. I was vulnerable to being taken over by aspects of others' interests and pursuits that I would typically disregard.

That state of affairs reminded me of the "old ones" talking about a woman they knew from the community who would walk up and down the street every day, obviously disturbed at her core; looking alive but absent from self: "She'll come to herself." They recognized the internal devastation and hopeful possibility of restoration.

I enjoyed disco roller skating. One day, a fellow skater who knew of my romantic relationship (they were social brothers) said to me when he was attempting to make an intimate entrance into my existence—he noticed the absence of my vibrant energy—"Never put all your eggs in one basket." He was speaking about the full extent of my bearings and direction emerging in the other person. I pondered that thought.

Subsequently, I learned a remedy that has withstood all acts and would have eradicated a personal, emotional reaction to the detriment of my "self"; the development of a standard; a meaningful principle for working through emotions:

- Only God does not change.

- The euphoric feelings derived from professions of the mouth are valid for the moment in which they are expressed.

- Trust God. Trust is confidence in His unconditional righteous love for me; an unwavering faith; an exercise in patience.

- Love men and women as God prescribed: "This is my commandment, That ye love one another, as I have loved you" (John 15:12).

- My response is not based on what someone does, but on biblical principles, especially the golden rule: "Therefore all things whatsoever ye would that men should do to you, do ye even so to them: for this is the law and the prophets" (Matt. 7:12).

"Put not your trust in princes, nor in the son of man, in whom there is no help" (Ps. 146:3). "There is a more reliable Protector and Helper than even the most noble of earth. Though princes be of royal blood they are but human. God alone merits our complete trust and confidence. Without Him we are helpless before many of the problems of life" (Nichol 1976, p. 936).

Much of the distress we experience as Christians comes not as the result of sin, but because we are ignorant of the laws of our nature. For instance, the only test we should use to determine whether or not to allow a particular emotion to run its course in our lives is to examine what the outcome of that emotion will be. Think it through to its logical conclusion, and if the outcome is something that God would condemn, put a stop to it immediately. However, if it is an emotion that has been kindled by the Spirit of God and you don't allow it to have its way in your life, it will cause a reaction on a lower level than God intended.

That is the way unrealistic and overly emotional people are made, and the higher the emotion, the deeper the level of corruption; it is not exercised on its intended level. If the Spirit of God has stirred you, make as many decisions as possible irrevocable, and let the consequences be what they will. "We cannot stay forever on the 'mount of transfiguration,' basking in the light of our mountaintop experience (see Mark 9:1–9), but we must obey the light we received there and put it into action. When God gives us a vision, we must transact business with Him at that point, no matter what the cost" (Chambers, March 22, 1992).

## The Third Element of Wellness Is Intellectual

Strong?

One biblical reference to the intellectual element is Philippians 2:5: "Let this mind be in you, which was also in Christ Jesus." This element pertains to one's mental capacity to comprehend ideas and relationships and exercise judgment.

I can recount times in my youth and young adulthood when people said, "You are a strong Black woman." I did not understand. I knew "strong" had to do with physical strength, so this was questionable for me. Then years later, I understood: strong in terms of my mind and convictions.

In the academic arena, educational institutions go through a standardization process, often referred to as accreditation/licensing. Those institutions that are awarded accreditation/licensing are recognized as distributing degrees that have met the criteria and standards established by authorizing entities. The educational institutions I attended met that qualification. As God would design, at the time I attended, financial aid was available, and there was no overt stigma for women with children to attend college.

When I started undergraduate school, I had one son and an absent husband. When I graduated with my doctorate, I had four children and an absent husband. For many of my adult years, I was a married, single mother. At the beginning of my college experience, I lived in the projects/city housing in the Bronx. When I completed my doctorate, I lived in a gated private cooperative in the Bronx. Much happened between the start of my college education and the finish, too numerous for the limits of this book. However, there are a few poignant observations.

College began for me during the era of "open admissions" in the City University of New York. Large numbers of students of color were admitted and eligible for state and federal financial aid. Socializing in college is where I learned to play the card game bid whist. It was a vertical campus in metropolitan New York, and students would gather in the student lounge. I would pass by it between classes or on break from my studies, always prioritizing going to class.

It was during my second year that I noticed the student lounge was almost empty during the usual high-volume periods. It was brought to my attention that nearly all the students who hung out in the student lounge, instead of going to class, were dismissed due to low grade point averages. Many years later, after I had completed my master's degree, I was at a dance and recognized a face I knew as an undergraduate. We spoke. He had been a star basketball player during my early college years. During the conversation, I learned that he never graduated from college and had since become a father.

> *Socializing and partying had been a big draw in my life, but it did not take the place of my goal of getting a college degree. It was embedded in me that "education is the key."*

Socializing and partying had been a big draw in my life, but it did not take the place of my goal of getting a college degree. It was embedded in me that "education is the key." For me, it is the key to a better life for me, my family, and the community. My blessing was to learn from my experiences and those of others to enhance my ability to accomplish my goals. Early on, I began the practice of creating boundaries to support my priorities. They have become fortified over the years.

One boundary was to prevent invasion into my family time. After a specified hour, I did not take telephone calls, except for an emergency. I used an answering machine on my phone. If a call came in after my prescribed time, I did not answer it. I could listen to the message. If it wasn't an emergency, I did not reply during my family time.

Also important was giving my children a sense of home, as I defined it. We had breakfast and dinner together. When they went to bed, I went to bed. If I was going to go out in the evening, I would inform them. I would spend my nights at home and be there in the mornings when I would wake them up for morning prayer and devotional story discussion, exercise, and breakfast. Every day, I would get up earlier than the children did and prepare for the day with my personal prayer, washing, and dressing before I woke them up in a peaceful manner.

Often, after going to bed in the evenings, I would wake up after a few hours and go to the bathroom to study and read. The bathroom was the only room with a door that offered privacy in the two-bedroom apartment, so I could turn on the light and not disturb the children while I prepared to be an academically proficient student.

There were constant "microaggressions," a term I read in an interview with Dr. Neil Degrasse Tyson, Director of the Hayden Planetarium in New York City. An excerpt from that interview encapsulates my drive: "And if you are susceptible to microaggressions, you would have left the field long ago. I was functionally immune to them, because my interest in the universe was broader and deeper than any possible negative force could have brought to bear on it" ("What Neil Degrasse Tyson Thinks Higher Education Gets Wrong," Chronicle of Higher Education, September 16, 2018). Clarity about my motivation withstood the obstacles that arose.

Microaggression and macroaggression activity came from every side of my universe, at different times, and often simultaneously: people who lived in my community, worked at my children's schools, attended my church; my family and coworkers; in the grocery store, department stores, and banks; from creditors, social agencies, hospitals, etc. Undeniably, people's perceptions drive their judgment and are embedded in the sum total of their experiences.

Even today in some communities there is a residue of tradition that women should not attend college or hold administrative positions, but only work to support their husbands' work. If there are children, the woman should be in the home, not out making a career. When the woman has four children as a married, single mother (like I did), the microaggressions become macroaggressions, outright acts of lack of support, especially when there was an obvious need and request.

There's a residue of "Who do you think you are?" and "I don't like you because ...." I maintained a sense of wholeness in this environment by keeping my business to myself, divulging personal information only on a need-to-know basis. Exercising these boundaries yielded a much better living experience for me. This strategy gave me clear passage as I advanced in my professional and social development.

## A Renewing of Your Mind. What Are You Thinking?

Change your thinking, change your life. "For as he thinketh in his heart, so is he" (Prov. 23:7). "Blessed be the Lord, who daily loadeth us with benefits, even the God of our salvation. Selah" (Ps. 68:19).

How do we come to know God's will? Paul told the Christians in Rome that they should "be not conformed to this world: but be ye transformed by the renewing of [their] mind" (Rom. 12:2). J.B. Phillips translates the first verb this way: "Don't let the world around you squeeze you into its own mould." All of us find ourselves under constant pressure to comply with what those who don't love Jesus do. Instead of succumbing to external pressures, we need to "let God re- make (us) so that (our) whole attitude of mind is changed" (Coffen 2009, p. 272).

"Finally, brethren, whatsoever things are true, whatsoever things *are* honest, whatsoever things *are* just, whatsoever things *are* pure; whatsoever things are lovely, whatsoever things *are* of good report; if *there be* any virtue, and if *there be* any praise, think on these things" (Phil. 4:8).

"Let this mind be in you, which was also in Christ Jesus" (2:5).

"A man's belly shall be satisfied with the fruit of his mouth; and with the increase of his lips shall he be filled. Death and life are in the power of the tongue: and they that love it shall eat the fruit thereof" (Prov. 18:20, 21).

## *What Value Have You Placed on Time Management? It Is Essential to Personal Development*

"But, beloved, be not ignorant of this one thing, that one day is with the Lord as a thousand years, and a thousand years as one day" (2 Pet. 3:8). "God is eternal. With Him there is no past, no future; all things are eternally present. He has no need for our limited concept of time, and we cannot confine Him or His ideas to our scale of days and years" (Nichol 1980, p. 614). However, within our realm of being regarding lifestyle management and personal development, there is a need for the structure of time as we know it: seconds, minutes, hours, days, months, and years.

If we were to tithe our time to the Lord, this would equate to two hours and twenty-four minutes a day, minimal. Busyness is not a sign of righteousness. Refer to Martha in the story portrayed in Luke 10. In making your decisions, measure what you do by asking this question: Where will your daily activities take you? To further inform the value of your time, invest in it so that you get from it the most in health, happiness, and success. The clock is running. Make the most of today.

During my college studies I was introduced to *The 7 Habits of Highly Effective People* by Stephen Covey. His third habit, put first things first, is a management habit to gain control of time and events in your life by seeing how they relate to your mission. There are two dimensions of this strategy to create categories of time demands: important and urgent. "Important" is attached to your roles and goals direction. "Urgent" is that which is pressing on you. Activities that are a waste of time are those not related to your mission.

In his work, there are four quadrants of time:

1. Urgent and important (problems, crises) needs to be attended to or you don't survive; major meeting to attend; without action, there is a major problem.

2. Not urgent and important—attached to mission; roles and goals, but without a sense of *now* about them.

3. Urgent not important—pressing, in front of you (i.e., unanswered mail); important to other people, not really attached to the overall mission.

4. Not urgent and not important—Time wasting, such as unprepared meetings, pleasant things—TV, unnecessary meetings, interruptions that can consume the entire day; busy all day, and at the end of the day, you feel like you accomplished nothing.

Additional time-management strategies:

1. The way we elect to spend our time determines the quality of our lives.

2. Sleeping periods should be at least one hour before midnight, at least four hours after midnight, and approximately a total of seven to eight hours per night.

3. Spend some time every day working toward realizing your important life goals.

4. Set priorities.

5. Identify multi-use of time (i.e., while doing the laundry, use the waiting time for exercise, playing with the child(ren), washing dishes, cleaning the stove, etc.).

6. Leave yourself a margin of safety and be flexible in case something unexpected needs to be addressed.

7. People respect your time when you demonstrate that you respect your time.

8. Time management gets better with practice and time.

9. For encouragement, reward yourself for each task accomplished.

10. Decide what's important to your vision and mission. Set boundaries and standards for the use of your time.

Consider, for your peace and the peace of those in your home, a need for rest. Set a boundary for accepting calls. Keep in mind a way of knowing when there is an emergency. Perhaps at a particular time in the evening and morning, let all calls go to voicemail or other message/answering service and listen to know when there is a situation you would consider an emergency. Otherwise, maintain the time boundary. This includes social media.

## The Fourth Element of Wellness Is Physical

There are many biblical references to the physical element. Read the examples below:

"For bodily exercise profiteth little: but godliness is profitable unto all things, having promise of the life that now is, and of that which is to come" (1 Tim. 4:8).

"Now Jacob's well was there. Jesus therefore, being wearied with his journey, sat thus on the well: and it was about the sixth hour. There cometh a woman of Samaria to draw water: Jesus saith unto her, Give me to drink" (John 4:6, 7).

"I beseech you therefore, brethren, by the mercies of God, that ye present your bodies a living sacrifice, holy, acceptable unto God, which is your reasonable service. And be not conformed to this world: but be ye transformed by the renewing of your mind, that ye may prove what is that good, and acceptable, and perfect, will of God" (Rom. 12:1, 2).

In the mornings, I incorporate a combination of spiritual and physical fitness. First is spiritual with morning prayers, Scripture reading, reciting verses from memory, and the reading of a Bible-based devotional short (one-page) story. I then engage in exercise. As a child, my father, who once served in the United States Army, would have my brother and me exercise as he continued to exercise at home after leaving the service.

Exercising is part of my daily routine. I would do all of the above before I woke up my children to follow the same pattern. The physical element pertains to the body—our material nature. "What? Know ye not that your body is the temple of the Holy Ghost *which is* in you, which ye have of God, and ye are not of your own? For ye are bought with a price: therefore glorify God in your body, and in your spirit, which are God's" (1 Cor. 6:19, 20). "Know ye not that ye are the temple of God, and *that* the Spirit of God dwelleth in you? If any man defile the temple of God, him shall God destroy; for the temple of God is holy, which *temple* ye are" (3:16, 17).

What do you allow into your body through your five senses: seeing, hearing, tasting, feeling, and smelling? The body has many parts that are each equally important. The following passage makes a spiritual application of a physical state of affairs:

> For the body is not one member, but many. If the foot shall say, Because I am not the hand, I am not of the body; is it therefore not of the body? And if the ear shall say, Because I am not the eye, I am not of the body; is it therefore not of the body? If the whole body *were* an eye, where *were* the hearing? If the whole *were* hearing, where *were* the smelling? But now hath God set the members every one of them in the body, as it hath pleased him. And if they were all one member, where *were* the body? But now *are they* many members, yet but one body. (1 Corinthians 12:14–20)

# *Lifestyle Management*

## The Fifth Element of Wellness Is Social

Many years ago, while attending a Prepaid Legal Services membership event in New York, I heard Tony Brown say that "man's payment for living on earth (rent) is to be in service to God." I agree that people are meant to be social and engage with each other. This service needs to be according to His standard. The social element pertains to the collective welfare, relationships, and living conditions of people in communities, exchanges with others, and social standards. Biblical references to this element include the following:

"Thou shalt not hate thy brother in thine heart: thou shalt in any wise rebuke thy neighbor, and not suffer sin upon him. Thou shalt not avenge, nor bear any grudge against the children of thy people, but thou shalt love thy neighbor as thyself: I *am* the Lord" (Lev. 19:17, 18).

*"The Son of man came eating and drinking, and they say, Behold a man gluttonous, and a winebibber, a friend of publicans and sinners. But wisdom is justified of her children.* (Matt. 11:19—refers to Jesus' friendliness toward humanity and open contact with sinners).

The social element pertains to the welfare, relationships, and living conditions of people collectively in communities. It is relational across roles and areas of responsibilities.

## A New Perspective on Life—Representation
## What You Do Always Counts

In America, one of the first battle cries from the colonies to the empire in England was, "No taxation without representation." The short version of this historical story is that this battle cry created a movement that led to the establishment of these United States of America. The principles that upheld this battle cry still exist; however, they are reconfigured in various forms, sundry ways, and will be for time eternal.

Representation is the undergirding for today's struggles. The expectation is that when you're represented, you will receive favor and privileges, merited or unmerited. Favorable consideration is an expectation, even an entitlement, because you're represented. Being represented means that your representative is a contributor to discussions that lead to decisions that impact the quality of your life.

Jesus is the Christians' representative before the throne of God (see Heb. 4:14–16, 7:25). Moses represented the people of Israel before Pharaoh, the head/leader of the Egyptian government (see Ex. 3:10). You represent your household, family, the community from which you come, and by extension, all people from your culture and ethnicity.

You are a role model and mentor, even on those occasions when it happens without anyone asking your permission to put you in that category. "Am I my brother's keeper" is a well-known retort from Cain (Gen. 4:9); absolutely you are! Draw the lesson from the standard Jesus set in the description of caring for others (see Matt. 25:31–46).

> *Jesus had a time of preparation. Moses had a time of preparation. You also can view your past level and degree of participation as a time of preparation and a learning experience that you will use as a foundation to propel forward in a determined effort to accept the responsibility of representation*

For persons now needing to take another look at their responsibilities for representing others, they must work toward a new understanding of their role as members of the human race (see Phil. 2:5, 12, 13, 15). Jesus had a time of preparation. Moses had a time of preparation. You also can view your past level and degree of participation as a time of preparation and a learning experience that you will use as a foundation to propel forward in a determined effort to accept the responsibility of representation—a responsibility that is unavoidable, and perhaps before now your acknowledgment may have been delayed.

Start this new perspective on life in your immediate surroundings: home, work, community. Participate in activities that contribute to the discussions that lead to decisions that have a positive impact. Frame your input in a way that will serve to constructively and progressively move decisions in the direction of improving the quality of your life and that of others.

In Luke 10:40–42, as I mentioned before, the application is that busyness is not a form of righteousness. The emphasis in Matthew 6:33 is to put God first. When you wake up in the morning, your first conversation is with God. Conversation also involves listening.

- Engagement as an employee/supervisor/administrator: "He hath shewed thee, O man, what *is* good; and what doth the Lord require of thee, but to do justly, and to love mercy, and to walk humbly with thy God?" (Mic. 6:8).

In all situations, do justly by God's standards. This means becoming familiar with Scripture and praying for the appropriate application thereof. A good companion to this practice is to ask God how to respond. This means you will also need to ask for recognition of His guidance and respond promptly to His leading.

As in the group setting that Jesus had early in His ministry, there were disciples throughout this period and at the last supper. Each one had a certain characteristic. These characteristics are likely to be in every group setting. You'll need to learn how to interact with each character at that particular time in your experience. Another observation is an excerpt from an intriguing article: "So never confuse your job with yourself" ("On Power, Charisma, and Showing Up: Advice to Rookie Presidents," The Chronicle of Higher Education, March 3, 2017). John Sexton, the transformative former president of New York University, once said that after a tough day, he would go home and read his business card, which said, "John Sexton, President." He would then remind himself that his critics were unhappy with what came after the comma; they knew very little about what came before.

- Engagement as a relative: "Behold, how good and how pleasant *it is* for brethren to dwell together in unity!" (Ps. 133:1).

There are boundaries. Become familiar with what they are; each relationship may differ. Be at peace. The fact that you are family does not change. What you have control over is your response to the relationship. There is loyalty in families, with different degrees and standards. You have a choice to exercise.

- Engagement with self (see Luke 10:40–42): "Therefore take no thought, saying, What shall we eat? or, What shall we drink? or, Wherewithal shall we be clothed? (For after all these things do the Gentiles seek:) for your heavenly Father knoweth that ye have need of all these things. But seek ye first the kingdom of God, and his righteousness; and all these things shall be added unto you" (Matt. 6:31–33). "In every thing give thanks: for this is the will of God in Christ Jesus concerning you" (1 Thess. 5:18). "And we know that all things work together for good to them that love God, to them who are the called according to *his* purpose" (Rom. 8:28).

- Engagement with others (see Prov. 3:27–30; Jer. 17:5–8):

Whenever I have flown in an airplane, the flight attendant would give instructions before taking off. They always included how to use the air mask, which would fall from the overhead area down in front of your seat under certain life-threatening circumstances. The instructions especially made note that you are to put the air mask on yourself before helping another person, even a child or infant. Help yourself first. Use God's standard and instructions in the process.

- Marriage is also a social engagement:

Marriage is thought to be about love. We know that God is love (see 1 John 4:8, 16). Therefore, guiding principles for sustaining a marriage may be found in the Bible.

"And the Lord God said, *It is* not good that the man should be alone; I will make him an help meet for him" (Gen. 2:18). The negative is extremely emphatic. It is not a construction to merely express a negative perception. In the context of chapters 1 and 2, Adam's initial solitude was the only thing "not good." After man and woman are completed, God said it was "very (exceedingly) good" (1:31). His plan for man was less than ideal and incomplete without woman, the emphasis being on "alone."

"Help" is a word frequently used in references to the Lord in the Psalms (e.g., 10:14; 22:11; 28:7; 46:1; 54:4; 72:12; 86:17; 119:173, 175; 121:1, 2, etc.).

Thus, it is not a degrading position for the woman. The verb form basically means to aid or supply that which the individual cannot provide for himself. It conveys the idea of aiding someone in need, such as the oppressed. A godly woman meets this need of man.

"'Meet' comes from the Hebrew word meaning 'opposite.' Literally, it is 'according to the opposite of him,' meaning that she will complement and correspond to him.

She is to be equal to and adequate for man. She is also made in the image of God, thus again, equal to man and not on the animal level" (King James Study Bible, Thomas Nelson Publishers, Nashville, 1988, pp. 10–11).

Life experiences impact the formation of a person's perspective. Saying the word "marriage" may either evoke thoughts of an endearing bond or disappointing separation in a relationship.

By the very nature of a marriage, a person transforms from a sense of self-importance to embracing a joining together to create an entity of one (see Gen. 2:24; Eph. 5:31).

Just like the human body, which has many parts with different essential functions, yet form one body, a marriage brings two people together into an entity of one. It takes time for the human body to develop. Thus, use the time to establish the bond as prescribed in Deuteronomy 24:5. In the context of today's living environment, the application of the timeframe in this verse would take the form of limiting activities to sustainable necessities and prioritizing the devotion of all your attention to the marriage. A husband-and-wife team is a powerful pillar of support for each other. Examples include the Honorable Judge Thurgood Marshall and Cecilia; the Honorable President Barack Obama and Michelle; Nabal and Abigail (see 1 Sam. 25:2); Joseph, the stepfather of Jesus, and Mary (see Matt. 1:16; Luke 1:27).

A major, guiding, biblical principle for sustaining a marriage centers on the submissiveness of both the husband and wife. "Wives, submit yourselves unto your own husbands, as unto the Lord. ... Husbands, love your wives, even as Christ also loved the church, and gave himself for it ... So ought men to love their wives as their own bodies. He that loveth his wife loveth himself" (Eph. 5:22, 25, 28). This lofty sacrifice of the husband is worthy of submission from the wife. Think of the Christ-and-church analogy. Jesus did not consider it robbery to be "born again." In a marriage, being born again is marked by a change in lifestyle. A wife should find it a delight to submit to the nurturing benevolence of a Christlike character in a husband (see v. 33; also 1 Peter 3:7). A caveat for the wife is to measure the husband's leadership/headship in the relationship by God's standard. "Wives, submit yourselves unto your own husbands, as it is fit in the Lord" (Col. 3:18).

Other biblical examples of marriage are Sarai/Sarah and Abram/Abraham (see Gen. 11:29); Adam and Eve (see 2:18, 21–24); Aquila and Priscilla (see Acts 18:2, 26; Rom. 16:3). Threads from their experiences can be found in present-day marriages.

Being a helpmeet undergirds the success of a marriage.

The memory of love given and received is the only gift that lasts a lifetime.

> *Jesus did not consider it robbery to be "born again." In a marriage, being born again is marked by a change in lifestyle. A wife should find it a delight to submit to the nurturing benevolence of a Christlike character in a husband*

- Engagement as a spouse (Eph. 5:25–33):

It takes time and commitment for a man and woman to become one in a spousal relationship. Verse 31 is pivotal in this passage: "For this cause shall a man leave his father and mother, and shall be joined unto his wife, and they two shall be one flesh" (see also Gen. 2:24; Matt. 19:5; Mark 10:7). However, Ephesians 5 gives context to how this is done in verses 23–25 and 32. The Christ element is essential.

There is a story I once heard. I'll offer my rendition as an example of commitment. One morning, on the road from the barn, a pig and a chicken caught up with each other as they walked toward the farmer's house. The pig said to the chicken, "Where are you going?"

The chicken said, "To the farmer's house for his breakfast. Where are you going?"

The pig replied, "To the farmer's house for his breakfast." Which one was committed (assuming bacon and eggs constitute a conventional breakfast)?

## Parenting

Everything created comes with instructions. Did you read the book before becoming a parent? Some people will get something new and begin to handle it, totally disregarding the instructions, just glad to get their new possession. Others will read the instructions and follow the guide provided by the manufacturer, creator, or inventor.

"God created man ... male and female created he them" (Gen. 1:27). The Bible is the resource on how to live, including being a parent. Remember, the acronym of B.I.B.L.E. is **B**asic **I**nstructions **B**efore **L**eaving **E**arth. Parenting lessons are embedded in the Scriptures, drawn from the stories of the lives of children's experiences, illustrated along the full range of the different stages of their development, such as Daniel, Hananiah, Mishael, and Azariah (see Dan. 1:8, 17–20); Joseph (see Gen. 30:1–12); a little maid (see 2 Kings 5:1–4); Timothy (see 2 Tim. 1:5, 3:15); Hannah (see 1 Samuel 1:10, 11); Jesus (see Luke 2:52); and others.

Elements portrayed in this book are essential to wellness in lifestyle management and personal development. A review of their lives reveals solid elements of spiritual, intellectual, physical, social, emotional, financial, and sexual standards. These stories give us insights into how to train up a child (see Prov. 22:6). There are ways to apply this instruction in the daily lives of yourself and your child(ren) (see 2 Tim. 3:16, 17).

Start your search for parenting guidance by identifying effective models. The original model for being a parent is God (see Matt. 6:9). His character includes sacrifice (see John 3:16, 17), inseparable commitment (see Rom. 8:38, 39), and discipline: "And ye have forgotten the exhortation which speaketh unto you as unto children, My son, despise not thou the chastening of the Lord, nor faint when thou art rebuked of him; (6) For whom the Lord loveth he chasteneth, and scourgeth every son whom he receiveth" (Heb. 12:5, 6).

Parents found in righteousness are leaders, whose examples, when followed by their child(ren), will lead to good standing in life. A parent's righteousness is measured by the degree to which God's principles are followed. For the most part, in revered parents can be found consistency and agreement between what they say and do. Parents without God's guidance practice, "Do what I say not what I do." In Christ, a parent nurtures and prepares for the child(ren) to live more abundantly and have peace and good stature with God and humanity.

Parenting is forever! What changes are the stages in development and application of age- and character-appropriate parenting interactions and interventions. Now is the time to get it right. Choose today which path your parenting will take. Consider Joshua's stand: ***"but as for me and my house, we will serve the Lord"*** (24:15).

## Personal Application

In our lives, there are relationships to which we respond, in essence as an obligation within our growth process. Engagement with others is inevitable. Determining your standards of operation is the "Why" of what you do and will always be a guide for "How" and "When" to do it. Remember, actions determine a person's character, particularly when in crisis.

We can choose to operate from a variety of standards, including historical, cultural, urban-influenced, socially nurtured, biblical, etc. For the purpose of this writing, the Bible is the standard for operating and engaging. Start implementing the new strategy for lifestyle management and personal development from the time you know to do differently. That will improve the quality of your life, family, and community. Be heavenly minded yet still of earthly good. The following passage highlights engagement as a parent:

> Hear, O Israel: The Lord our God *is* one Lord: And thou shalt love the Lord thy God with all thine heart, and with all thy soul, and with all thy might. And these words, which I command thee this day, shall be in thine heart: And thou shalt teach them dili-

gently unto thy children, and shalt talk of them when thou sittest in thine house, and when thou walkest by the way, and when thou liest down, and when thou risest up. And thou shalt bind them for a sign upon thine hand, and they shall be as frontlets between thine eyes. And thou shalt write them upon the posts of thy house, and on thy gates. (Deuteronomy 6:4–9)

A parent is one who begets, gives birth to, or nurtures and raises a child, according to *The American Heritage College Dictionary*. When is a parent no longer a parent? Even in death, you are referred to as the mother or father of your child(ren). Remember, people talk about their memories of their parent(s) or refer to their training and childhood experiences. In a child's life, the parent is the parent regardless of status or the depth of the relationship. What changes is the degree of your overt relationship as both you and the child(ren) move through stages of development.

## Implementation of a Nurturing Standard

First, practice the instructions in your own life. With your children, in an age-appropriate way, start the day with prayer, reading a Bible verse and related short story (some refer to this as devotional readings), and soliciting or offering the meaning of the verse and Bible story for personal application and understanding. I understand the King James Version of the Holy Bible is written on an eighth-grade reading level. Children's intellectual abilities are enhanced by listening and reading at the grade level of the book.

Also, ensure they have their breakfast to sustain them during the day and incorporate a short exercise regimen, such as five push-ups, stretching, etc. All of this engagement should occur before leaving for school on time. This may require an adjustment in your choices to accommodate improvements in your lifestyle and personal management.

## Parenting Through the Different Stages of Development (Parenting 101)

This information is intended to provide you with an overview of the different stages of development. Remember, no two persons have the same makeup or needs. The comments are designed to help parents gain insight into the vast array of social dynamics, which take place simultaneously during an individual's lifetime from childhood through adulthood.

Exercise your right and responsibility to ask appropriate persons for assistance concerning specific problems. People have different values and standards for daily living. Make sure your resource person exemplifies the qualities of life you want to emulate.

Here are some Scriptural references that reflect the movement from childhood to adulthood:

> "When I was a child, I spake as a child, I understood as a child, I thought as a child: but when I became a man, I put away childish things" (1 Cor. 13:11).

> "Train up a child in the way he should go: and when he is old, he will not depart from it" (Prov. 22:6).

> "Children, obey your parents in the Lord: for this is right. Honour thy father and mother; which is the first commandment with promise; That it may be well with thee, and thou mayest live long on the earth. And, ye fathers, provoke not your children to wrath: but bring them up in the nurture and admonition of the Lord" (Eph. 6:1–4).

> *Exercise your right and responsibility to ask appropriate persons for assistance concerning specific problems. People have different values and standards for daily living. Make sure your resource person exemplifies the qualities of life you want to emulate.*

### *Thought-Provoking Questions:*

1. Which biblical characters' parenting skills would you have liked to experience or practice?

2. What lessons are learned from their experiences?

*Remember: We can learn from everyone and everything, either what to do or what not to do!*

- Abraham
- Sarah
- The parents of Daniel
- The parents of Naaman's wife's young maid
- Timothy's grandmother
- Rahab
- Joseph
- Aaron
- Mary
- Samuel's mother
- Jacob
- Job
- Naomi
- Others

# Some Characteristics of the Stages of Development: Age, Phase, and Christian Nurturing Activities

| AGE | PHASE OF DEVELOPMENT | CHRISTIAN NURTURING ACTIVITIES |
|---|---|---|
| Prenatal (1 week to birth) | Choosing a doctor | Healthy choices: food, music, environment |
| Infancy (1 to 11 months) | Big smile, emerging personality | Hearing the Word of God, singing, reading |
| Toddler (12 to 24 months) | Whirlwind of activity | Praying with you, looking at picture books, listening to Christian stories |
| Pre-school (3 to 5 years) | Self-reliant, leaving the nest | Christian environment at home, early morning and evening prayer, reading devotional stories daily |
| Primary school (6 to 9 years) | A big first grader | Reading Bible stories, morning and evening family prayers |
| Pre-teen (10 to 12 years) | Pre-adolescent | Prayer, sharing living examples of God's standard discussions |
| Puberty (12 years) | Declaration of independence | Family prayer, love notes of encouragement |
| Adolescence (13 to 18 years) | Age of rapid changes, friends, clothes, music, and more | Prayer, devotional stories, structural activities |
| **Adulthood** | | |
| 18 to 22 years | Leaving home | Mailing tracts, sending inspiration cards |
| 23 to 28 years | Moving into the adult world | Scheduling time together, prayer |
| 29 to 34 years | Search for stability | Invitations to church programs, prayer, inspirational gifts: CDs, DVDs, books |

| AGE | PHASE OF DEVELOPMENT | CHRISTIAN NURTURING ACTIVITIES |
|---|---|---|
| 35 to 42 years | Becoming one's own person | Expressions of love |
| 43 to 55 years | Settling down | Love notes: texts, cards, creating special traditional dates |
| 56 to 64 years | The mellowing | Scripture reading, devotional stories, traditional dates of remembrance |
| 65+ years | Life review | Inclusion, expressions of love |

"Train up a child in the way he should go: and when he is old, he will not depart from it" (Prov. 22:6).

"And it was so, when the days of *their* feasting were gone about, that Job sent and sanctified them, and rose up early in the morning, and offered burnt offerings *according* to the number of them all: for Job said, It may be that my sons have sinned, and cursed God in their hearts. Thus did Job continually" (Job 1:5).

To dos:

- "Parents should reflect on their interactions with their children to analyze the values they instill in them. They should assess their attitudes or decisions during situations and evaluate them according to the long-term effects they may have on the child's own personality. Parents should also reflect on their actions after situations to see if their behavior was appropriate for the situation" (Leigh M. O'Brien, "Reflecting parenting," *Childhood Education*, Summer 1996, v. 72, n. 4, p. 238).

- Parents should desist from saying things that would hurt their children's feelings and destroy their self-esteem. Instead, they should use constructive criticism and praise to boost their children's confidence (Harriet Webster, "Seven things smart parents never say," *Readers Digest*, Feb. 1996, v. 148 n. 886, p. 25).

- The words parents use to censure their children can affect their self-image. Five common words and phrases a parent should never use are: "Why can't you?"; "You're a spoiled brat"; "Who started it?" (referring to sibling fights); "If you don't"; and "never," "ever," or "always" (Nancy Samalin and Donna Brown Hogarty, *Parents Magazine*, March 1995, v. 70 n. 3, p. 37). Other examples: "You always leave your junk around"; "You never obey us." Instead, phrase corrections in specific positive terms.

- Many experts state that reading to one's children for a few minutes every day not only stimulates their imagination but encourages them to read as well. Reading to children helps instill in their minds the idea that reading is a fun activity and not work. It is one of the most important things you can do for your child (David M. Schwartz, *Reader's Digest*, July 1995, v. 147 n. 879, p. 163).

- People who have children should commit to raising those children. Parents should try to give their children a sense of family, even if the family is not perfect. It may be many years before the rewards of child-rearing become apparent (Frank Pittman, *Psychology Today*, May–June 1995, v. 28 n. 3, p. 42).

- Pre-teens often chose friends who might appear strange to their parents. The latter must refrain from prejudging these friends, and when disapproval is expressed, it must be done gently. Still, parents must set limits on what their children and their friends do together (Anne C. Bernstein, March 1995, v. 70 n. 3, p. 95 [3]).

- Some parents tend to belittle the problem that is causing hurt feelings in their children, but children benefit more when their parents listen actively and understand the problem from the child's perspective. Parents should let their children know that bad feelings are okay, but bad behavior is not (Nancy Samalin and Catherine Whitney, *Parents Magazine*, Feb. 1995, v. 70 n. 2, p. 49 [3]).

- Parents make a mistake when they try too hard to be friends with their children. Parents can maintain proper control by acting as leaders, being consistent in disciplinary measures, emphasizing good behavior, and not allowing their children to use their first names (*USA Today* (magazine), May 1994, v. 122 n. 2588, p. 9 [1]).

- By giving a toddler several choices, a power struggle can be avoided. Parents should also avoid shaming a toddler (J. Ronald Lally, *Parents Magazine,* March 1994, v. 69 n. 3, p. 76 [3]).

- Modeling desired behavior is better than physical discipline. Rules should be fair and consistent (*USA Today* (magazine), Jan. 1994, v. 122 n. 2584, p. 9 [1]).

- Teaching good behavior is more about showing than telling. Discipline – a process of learning and guidance that is based on respect for your child. Base decisions about managing your child's behavior on your understanding of his/her interests, preferences, needs, and concerns. S/he begins to sense the care and regard that you have for him/her. As a result, the child develops the same kind of respect for you and wants to behave in ways that please you ("Discipline with respect," *Parents Magazine*, Feb. 1995, v. 70 n. 2, p. 72 [2]).

- Say "Tell me something you learned in science today" instead of "How was school today?"

It is important to exercise this engagement in a peaceful environment. Eliminate the shouting and increase the acts of approval and encouragement. The living environment will become nurturing. In the evenings, let the last engagement as a family be prayer.

There were certain parenting activities that I executed during later stages of my children's development. As children grow, they are often out of the home and eventually move out. Continue the biblical connection and guidance throughout these stages. With technology, send early morning texts with short biblical references and cell photos of devotional readings. You might also give them a book each year with biblical stories and references.

Select a Bible verse that speaks to your blessing for them. Share the verse with each child and reference it in each conversation and as a closing remark and blessing for the child's wellness. Every individual has his or her own characteristics to nurture, so select a different Bible verse for each child. There are also verses to apply generally. Also, offer a personal one based on the parental insights gained through your engagement with them.

Children's home training is essential. Examine the following references:

1. Can we sing in a foreign land? Yes, praise God at all times (see Ps. 137:4)! "But as for you, ye thought evil against me; *but* God meant it unto good, to bring to pass, as *it is* this day, to save much people alive" (Gen. 50:20).

2. 2 Kings 5:3; "Although a captive, the maid did not forget her homeland or her God. Nor did she think thoughts of ill toward those who had taken her captive and forced her into an involuntary servitude. Filled with love toward her God, her heart went out in sympathy to her ailing master and his wife. Instead of wishing Naaman ill because of the misfortunes that had been brought upon her, she wished him well and hoped for his recovery from his terrible disease. Remembering the marvelous works of Elisha in her homeland, she had faith that the prophet could heal Naaman of his leprosy. What God had brought through His servant in Israel, she believed He could also perform toward those of an alien race" (Nichol 1976, p. 875).

3. Daniel, Shadrach, Meshach, and Abednego; *"**Among these.** This expression shows that other young men were selected for training in addition to the four mentioned by name. These four are doubtless mentioned because of the uniqueness of their experience. Their unwavering loyalty to God earned for them great rewards in worldly honor and spiritual blessing"* (Nichol 1976, p. 759).

4. While they are away from you, whether through daily activities, leaving home, or long- term separation, the Bible they learned at home will carry them for life. When you separate in the morning, you don't know how or when you will come back together.

Elements of this training:

a. Prayer

b. Diet—eating; the selection of food

c. Etiquette—good manners; company of kings

Parenting is forever. What changes is how you interact in the different stages of life. Both parents and child(ren) move through stages of development differently and at different times. What doesn't change is your responsibility as a parent. Measure everything by the standard you've chosen for living and keep it in context.

Regarding a passage like Deuteronomy 6:6–9, I can hear someone say, "Those were ancient times! How do you do that now?" I'm glad the person asked. There is a practical application for the here and now.

In the mornings, repeat and even read a Bible verse together. Hard to do with your schedule and lifestyle? Get up a little earlier each day, since God doesn't sleep (see Ps. 121:3, 4). He's always available to receive your thoughts directed toward heaven.

For parents with children out of the house, living on their own, text or e-mail them a Scripture that will uplift them regardless of their situation.

As quietly as it's kept, to speak Scripture, you will need to know Scripture. Read the Bible. It does a multitude of good.

## The Sixth Element of Wellness Is Finance

The sixth element of wellness in lifestyle management and personal development is finance. The financial element pertains to the management of money and other resources.

"Thus saith the Lord, thy Redeemer, the Holy One of Israel; I *am* the Lord thy God which teacheth thee to profit, which leadeth thee by the way *that* thou shouldest go" (Isa. 48:17).

"Labour not to be rich: cease from thine own wisdom. Wilt thou set thine eyes upon that which is not? For riches certainly make themselves wings; they fly away as an eagle toward heaven" (Prov. 23:4, 5).

"But thou shalt remember the Lord thy God: for it is he that giveth thee power to get wealth, that he may establish his covenant which he sware unto thy fathers, as it is this day" (Deut. 8:18).

"A feast is made for laughter, and wine maketh merry: but money answereth all things" (Eccles. 10:19).

> *God's math is different from humanity's math.*

God's math is different from humanity's math. One story comes to mind. On one of the occasions I applied for welfare—or it may have been a recertification appointment—I was denied. In preparation for the appointment, I went over the math of all my finances and expenses. It was evident to me that I needed additional financial assistance. When I met with the representative, her numbers showed I had a surplus. This couldn't be, based on my calculations. I automatically calculated the tithe and offering I was returning to the church. The welfare regulations did not count tithe as a living expense. I left the office. God provided, even with the denial of the welfare benefits I was requesting.

Regarding money basics, do you know the answers to the questions below? Can you answer these questions right now at the reading of this statement? Hmm. Knowing this information about your money matters is a good position from which to orchestrate your financial growth.

- How much cash do you have on your person right now (wallet, pocket, bag, etc.)?
- If you have credit, what is the highest interest rate you are currently paying for your debt or credit?
- How much money do you spend on any given day?
- If you pay off your debts, do you have a credit score? Credit is evaluated on your payment history, such as making payments on time.
- What is the difference between living expenses and debt?

The following elements of money management comprise the first steps in creating a foundation from which to position yourself to attract more money in the form of assets, credit, collateral, and property:

1. Faithfully return a tithe and give an offering to the church.
2. Faithfully pay your financial debts. It is more important to pay it when it is due than to delay it.
3. You must spend money to get money. Wisely incur debt that you can manage in a way that the record shows payment on time and a credit line with more than half the credit available for use.

4. Maintain at least four sources of credit in good standing.

5. Write down your expenditures each day. Keep a record.

6. Write down the amount of money you receive each month (income).

7. Make adjustments on how you spend money, using the information you wrote down about your spending and income (refer to numbers 5 and 6 above).

8. Save money consistently and systematically.

    a. Be patient with solidifying the financial adjustments you want to make. Give yourself about two years to establish a financial record that indicates good character. In financial matters, "good character" is determined by your credit history. Credit history is determined by your profile of borrowing and paying back the money under the terms of the agreement for which you were extended credit.

9. Return the payments for your credit in advance of the due date. When the payment arrives after the due date, it is a late payment. Late payments are less favorable than payments made on or before the due date.

10. Always receive proof of satisfaction of payment or a statement that says "paid in full" from the creditor when you close an account.

    Paperwork can work for or against you. Keep your records of loan and credit agreements and the payment history in a safe, accessible location.

When you've mastered the above, you are handling your money matters.

## A New Perspective on Wealth

Wealth is about more than just money. I heard it said, "Money isn't everything, but it is right up there with oxygen." Wealth is a means to material gain. It is the ability to make valuable exchanges. In addition to money, wealth comes in the form of influences: a person recognized for his or her sense of fairness, moral standards, accountability, and accessibility to clients, customers, and associations; a family that is in one accord, supportive, in agreement with each other, and healthy. This sense of wealth is exemplified when solely on a person's "word," business is transacted, favor is extended, arrangements are secured, etc.

Solomon, the richest man who ever lived, began his status of wealth the moment he made a request of God for wisdom and knowledge. The king desired these attributes for use in judging and working with people. "Wisdom and knowledge is granted unto thee; and I will give thee riches, and wealth, and honor, such as none of the kings have had that have been before thee, neither shall there any after thee have the like" (2 Chron. 1:12).

Consider that money can't buy you health; otherwise, a lot of rich people would still be alive. As quietly as it's kept, you need health to get wealth. Everything you do on the journey to acquiring wealth does count. The result doesn't necessarily justify the means.

Building character is what will make a person wealthy. Think of character as a reputation, distinguishing trait, or quality. Your character gets developed by the choices you make.

Your _character_ is determined by the _words_ you feed on and allow to influence your _thinking_, which in turn triggers your _emotions_, which then becomes the basis for your _decisions_, which is what shapes your _actions_. However, these actions when repeated becomes a _habit_, which then forms your _character_ (Dr. Creflo Dollar, Pastor, World Changers Church, Georgia and New York, emphasis added).

Our choices determine the quality of our lives. Each day we are provided with a new opportunity for decisions that will work to our benefit or detriment. "Blessed be the Lord, who daily loadeth us with benefits, even the God of our salvation. Selah" (Ps. 68:19). Let the standard for making choices be Matthew 6:33: "But seek ye first the kingdom of God, and his righteousness; and all these things shall be added to you."

"Every man also to whom God hath given riches and wealth, and hath given him power to eat thereof, and to take his portion, and to rejoice in his labour; this *is* the gift of God (Eccles. 5:19).

"Receive my instruction, and not silver; and knowledge rather than choice gold. For wisdom is better than rubies; and all the things that may be desired are not to be compared to it" (Prov. 8:10, 11).

Consider a value-added exchange, a purchase greater than finance: "Fear not: for I have redeemed thee, I have called *thee* by thy name: thou *are* mine" (Isa. 43:1).

In general, purchases require money. You exchange money, the cost of the item, to purchase the desired possession. There are substitutes for money in the purchase of food. For example, food stamps are redeemed for the food items you desire.

There is a cost for everything. In your relationship with God, you sacrifice (cost) your natural tendencies for spiritual acts of worship, a living offering holy and pleasing to God. "Behold, I was shapen in iniquity; and in sin did my mother conceive me" (Ps. 51:5) Yet, we develop our character through the redemption of Christ Jesus. "Who gave himself for us, that he might redeem us from all iniquity, and purify unto himself a peculiar people, zealous of good works" (Titus 2:14).

"Thus saith the Lord, thy Redeemer, the Holy One of Israel; I am the Lord thy God which teacheth thee to profit, which leadeth thee by the way that thou shouldest go" (Isa. 48:17).

Managing your money must be intentional. It is a process and may take time to arrive at a financial goal. Decide and acknowledge what your relationship is with money (see 1 Tim. 6:10). Do you know, at any given time, how much money you have on your person? When you're interested in purchasing something, do you calculate the impact of its amount on your ability to keep your current expenses paid on time? Do you give money away? Have you made a plan to decrease your debt? Do you have a plan for the use of an increase in income? Do you know your cash flow?

Cash flow = income – expenses. Include, in the calculation of your expenses, entertainment, vacations/staycations, and gifts. If your debt exceeds your desire, exercise ways to get to a manageable level of debt. Some actions may be to stop accumulating debt by identifying its cause, create a stick-to-it budget (how much you will spend on a category of expenses), use cash/ATM card as much as possible and credit cards for emergencies only.

Here's a model for managing finance that I like. Perhaps this information will be useful to you.

- Chart all of your debt: the name, amount owed, interest rate, and monthly payment.

- You can either choose to pay off the item/debt with the highest interest rate first or pay in full the debt with the least amount owed.

- Whichever debt you select, make a plan for how you'll pay it off while continuing to keep your other payments current when possible.

- Once you pay off one debt in full, you'll have that monthly payment available for other uses.

- Save money, even if you start with the small change in your pocket.

- Daily notate your expenditures: gas, candy, lunch, newspaper, etc.

- Every month, review your expenditures and determine how much you spent on incidentals and what, if any, you will adjust.

- As you patiently endure (which develops your strength of character), your long-term goals will produce long-term growth.

- It took a moment to get into debt. It takes more time to get out of debt.

Wealth is an abundance of valuable material possessions or resources, all of which have value in terms of exchange or use, according to the Merriam-Webster Dictionary (1997). A more practical definition is "An income that continueth to come whether thou work or travel" (Scott 2006, p. 44).

The first step to gain wealth is to answer the following two questions: 1) Wealth for what purpose? I've heard of people winning the lottery and being broke without money or possessions or funds within a few years; 2) What is your plan for obtaining wealth? The second step is to have a vision, which is required. Vision is a precise, clearly defined goal with a detailed plan and timetable for achieving it (see Scott 2006, p. 33).

The next phase is to conduct some basic housekeeping tasks, so to speak, and make an assessment of your current situation. "For which of you, intending to build a tower, sitteth not down first, and counteth the cost, whether he have *sufficient* to finish *it*" (Luke 14:28)?

"Now therefore thus saith the Lord of hosts; *Consider your ways*. Ye have sown much, and bring in little; ye eat, but ye have not enough; ye drink, but ye are not filled with drink; ye clothe you, but there is none warm; and he that earneth wages earneth wages *to put it* into a bag with holes" (Hag. 1:5, 6, emphasis in v. 5 added).

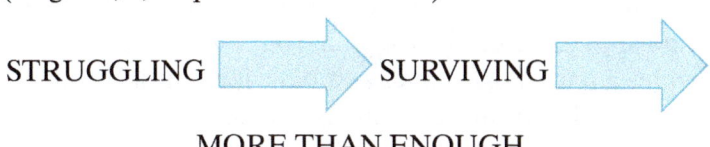

STRUGGLING → SURVIVING →

MORE THAN ENOUGH

Where are you on the above continuum? And where do you want to be? One lesson from the book *The Richest Man in Babylon* would be to budget using nine-tenths of your income. Additionally, "One may not condemn a man for succeeding because he knows how" (p. 35). "Control thy expenditures" (p. 40) and "BUDGET" (p. 41).

"What each of us calls our necessary expenses will always grow to equal our incomes unless we protest to the contrary.

1. Make a list of each thing you desire

2. Select those that are necessary and others that are possible through the expenditure of nine tenths of thy income.

3. Cross out the rest and consider them but a part of that great multitude of desires that must go unsatisfied and regret them not.

4. Budget then thy necessary expenses. Touch not the one tenth that is fattening they purse. Let this be thy great desire that is being fulfilled.

Desires must be simple and definite. They defeat their own purpose should they be too many, too confusing, or beyond a man's training to accomplish" (p. 52).

I thought of another way to budget income increases. I remember reading an article in *Essence* magazine where a woman was able to purchase a real estate property by saving all the increases she earned and living on her base, original salary. This is a good example of budgeting.

## A New Perspective on Life: When You Have a J.O.B.

Are you the one working your way up the career ladder? positioned at the bottom level in the company hierarchy? or sandwiched in a mid-level position, perhaps even working at a temporary assignment? At this job, what is it that you do?

For some, a J.O.B. positions them to be financially **Just-Over-Broke**. There are some who consider themselves under-compensated for the value they bring to the organization. Whatever your situation, know that what you do speaks for or against you. Your consistency in your performance creates a record that serves as a basis for your job evaluation. The guidance we receive from Scripture is, "Whether therefore ye eat, or drink, or whatsoever ye do, do all to the glory of God" (1 Cor. 10:31).

There are rules in each workplace, written and unwritten. The written rules you agree to follow when you accept the job: be on time, fulfill your position's responsibilities, etc. The unwritten rules, when violated, can stifle your advancement. The old saying holds true: "You are judged by the company you keep." There is no escaping that fact of life.

> *My mother would say, "Whatever you become, be a good one, whether you're a toilet bowl cleaner or the person in charge." My father would say, "Whatever work you do, do it good enough to put your name on it." Produce quality.*

Knowing the unwritten rules or not, you are still responsible. However, there are some general realities to guide you through the unknown rules in the workplace: 1) Regardless of your title or role in the company, you are responsible for your actions; 2) There isn't a title or position in existence for which a company's indemnification protocol relieves you of the consequences of your actions. This rule holds true in the natural and spiritual aspects of life. "But he that doeth wrong shall receive for the wrong which he hath done: and there is no respect of persons" (Col. 3:25); 3) Maintain the context of the roles of employer, supervisor, employee, etc. Don't mix them up. These roles define the relationship. The relationship changes when the roles change.

My mother would say, "Whatever you become, be a good one, whether you're a toilet bowl cleaner or the person in charge." My father would say, "Whatever work you do, do it good enough to put your name on it." Produce quality. Life proves that the combination of what you do and say defines your character. People watch to see a sermon in action. Those who are faithful in fulfilling their job responsibilities position themselves for advancement. A powerful statement about faithfulness is Luke 19:17: *"And he said unto him, Well, thou good servant: because thou hast been faithful in a very little, have thou authority over ten cities."*

In the J.O.B. market, you also position yourself for advancement by being of *added value* to the organization. You become of *added value* when you learn as much as you can, volunteer and accept additional responsibilities, and work with others to get a job done that will help the company. As a point of caution, the additional assignments are appreciated only when you can do them without neglecting your primary work responsibilities.

Compensation for these additional tasks comes in the form of money and knowledge. In some cases, the money might not come at the moment of executing the additional tasks. Nevertheless, your knowledge base will increase, which will make you of *added value* to the company. In the business world, monetary compensation follows knowledge.

Keep in mind that while you are positioning yourself for advancement, health can get you wealth, but wealth cannot get you health. Wisely choose how you use the God-given resource of life. A J.O.B.—**J**ust-**O**ver-**B**roke— is a beginning to having more than enough. God is omni-resourceful. I am a living witness and testimony of His goodness.

## The Seventh Element of Wellness Is Sexual

The seventh element of wellness in lifestyle management and personal development is sexual. The sexual element pertains to the attraction of one for another; relations; intercourse. "So God created man in his own image, in the image of God created he him; man and female created he them. And God blessed them, and God said unto them, Be fruitful, and multiply, and replenish the earth, and subdue it: and have dominion over the fish of the sea, and over the fowl of the air, and over every living thing that moveth upon the earth" (Gen. 1:27, 28).

At some point in biology class, you learn that during the act of sexual intercourse, thousands of sperm travel through the birth canal to get to one egg from a woman's ovary. The first sperm to arrive and penetrate the egg is what constitutes pregnancy. The sperm carries characteristics of the donor. Once intercourse takes place, it leaves some degree of impressionable remnants in and on each person.

Evidently, there is more to sex than the moment. It stands to reason that each time the act occurs, it is actually with the remnants of every person with whom both people have had relations. For example, if one person receives a disease from another and then has sexual intercourse with someone else, all three now have the disease.

Sex is good with appropriate boundaries.

## A New Perspective on Love

Love is a living principle, not an emotion! It doesn't waiver, depending on the circumstances. It's a strong force that endures. Love is of a heavenly origin. It is sacred and to be cultivated for the honor and glory of God. It makes itself known in acts of kindness: speaking tender, true, and encouraging words and offering oneself for the other person's well-being and salvation. The greatest sacrifice in a love relationship is when a person lays down his or her life for another person (see John 15:13).

> *Love is a living principle, not an emotion!*

God is love (see 1 John 4:8, 16) and the heavenly originator thereof. Love is expressed in John 3:16–17: "For God so loved the world, that he gave his only begotten Son, that whosoever believeth in him should not perish, but have everlasting life. For God sent not his Son into the world to condemn the world; but that the world through him might be saved."

In your relationship, what part of your character and which of your ways are you willing to give up, let die, or discontinue, purely as an expression of love? Is there something you need to do differently that will change your habits, thoughts, and behavior? When you love the Lord, you give up your life as you know it as a sacrifice in order to be born again. When you arrive at the state of loving, you change your ways according to God's standard. Love is a powerful force sufficient enough to bring you into the right relationship with someone.

The implosion of a love experience cannot be contained. It flows, overflows, and seeks a way to return the love. The way to do that is stated in Deuteronomy 6:5: "And thou shalt love the Lord thy God with all thine heart, and with all thy soul, and with all thy might." "We love him, because he first Loved us" (1 John 4:19).

True to human development, love involves a growth process. Whatever your age, when you decide to love, it brings on a new-birth experience. It is new growth, as exemplified by moving away from old behaviors that act against the love that has been given to you.

Nobody is born fully grown. Like little children, you take those first steps; you stumble or fall. When that happens, the parent tells the child, "You can do it," "Get back up," or "I'll give you a hand." The child gets back up and takes more steps. When the child tries again, the parent will applaud and embrace the child, showing approval and love. In time and with practice, the child walks with less-frequent falls and gets stronger and more determined.

It is the same in your walk of love in righteousness. Your growth in the area of relationships with others progresses from the place of being a babe—a child of God—to the place of being a man or woman of God. Love will move you through all the phases of your development.

We should love each other as God has loved us. Love is undefeatable.

Who shall separate us from the love of Christ? *shall* tribulation, or distress, or persecution, or famine, or nakedness, or peril, or sword? ... Nay, in all these things we are more than conquerors through him that loved us. For I am persuaded, that neither death, nor life, nor angels, nor principalities, nor things present, nor things to come, Nor height, nor depth, nor any other creature, shall be able to separate us from the love of God, which is in Christ Jesus our Lord. (Romans 8:35, 37–39)

This principle of inseparable, righteous love is further illustrated in the poem "Foot Prints" (authorship disputed). The last paragraph states, "The Lord said unto him, 'My precious, precious child, I love you and would never leave you. During your times of trial and tribulation, when you see only one set of foot prints, it was then that I carried you.'"

Don't get it twisted. Love is about life, not acts that rob you of your wellbeing. **"*I am come that they might have life, and that they might have* it *more abundantly*"** (John 10:10).

## In Reflection

Work environments vary—people, locations, products, etc. Given you must work to sustain some semblance of a quality of life, you venture out into the unknown. You start like a *Star Wars* episode, entering mysterious worlds, places, and positions with which you haven't had prior exposure or experience. This happens each time you enter the world of work and change your job or position. Like the *Star Wars* episode, you will survive and live to embark on a new adventure when you follow prescribed standards for operating.

One constant that will keep you sustained in the employment arena is navigating the processes and systems of the institution, undergirded by a standard of operation—integrity and righteousness—with an effectiveness that will withstand scrutiny. Your guiding light in this unknown arena must be the compass of the Holy Spirit within you—the place within you from which you draw your strength.

Knowing who you are and Whose you are will formulate your presentation at all times. You are wonderfully and marvelously made—God's creation. You are not a mistake! You are most valuable and have not yet arrived at all that you will be. Stay encouraged. You are redeemed to choose the standard and quality of life you want to live.

The foundation for all your resources is in a relationship with God. As your ancestors did, pray often and learn the truths in the Bible and their practical applications in your life. May God's force be with you.

# *Bibliography*

Brown, Claude. *Manchild in the Promised Land*. New York/Toronto: The Macmillan Company/Collier-Macmillan Canada, 1965.

Brown, Tony. *Empower the People*. New York: William Morrow and Company Publishers, 1998.

Chambers, Oswald. *My Utmost for His Highest*. Grand Rapids, MI: Discovery House, 1992.

Christenson, Jenny. "Making the Mind-Body Connection," *Counseling Today*, February 2009, pages 24-29..

*Chronicle of Higher Education*, September 21, 2018.

Clason, George S. *The Richest Man in Babylon*. New York: Penguin Group, 1955.

Coffen, Richard W. *Snapshots of God*. Hagerstown, MD: Review & Herald Publishing Association, 2009.

Covey, Stephen. *7 Habits of Highly Effective People*. New York: Simon & Schuster, 1989.

David M. Schwartz, *Reader's Digest*, July 1995, v. 147 n. 879, p. 163.

"Discipline with Respect." *Parents Magazine*, February 1995.

Douglass, Herbert. *Believe His Prophets*. Nampa, ID: Pacific Press, 2015.

Jakes, T.D. *Repositioning Yourself: Living Life Without Limits*. New York: Atria Books, 2007.

King James Study Bible. Nashville, TN: Thomas Nelson Publishers.

Lapin, Rabbi Daniel. *Thou Shall Prosper: Ten Commandments for Making Money*. Hoboken, NJ: John Wiley & Sons. Inc., 2002.

Nichol, Francis D., ed. *The Seventh-day Adventist Bible Commentary*, vol. 2. Hagerstown, MD: Review and Herald Publishing Association, 1954.

Nichol, Francis D., ed. *The Seventh-day Adventist Bible Commentary*, vol. 4. Hagerstown, MD: Review and Herald Publishing Association, 1955.

Nichol, Francis D., ed. *The Seventh-day Adventist Bible Commentary*, vol. 7. Hagerstown, MD: Review and Herald Publishing Association, 1957.

O'Brien, Leigh M. "Reflecting Parenting," *Childhood Education* 72, no. 4 (Summer 1996).

"On Power, Charisma, and Showing Up: Advice to Rookie Presidents," *The Chronicle of Higher Education*, March 3, 2017.

"Parent." *The American Heritage College Dictionary*, 3rd ed. CITY: Houghton Mifflin Co., 2000.

Pittman, Frank. *Psychology Today*, May–June 1995.

"Refreshed." *Oxford American Dictionary*. New York: Oxford University Press, 1980.

Robinson, Christy K., ed. *We Shall Be Changed: A Devotional from Quiet Hour Ministries*. Hagerstown, MD: Review & Herald Publishing Association, 2010.

Samalin, Nancy and Catherine Whitney. *Parents Magazine*, February 1995.

Samalin, Nancy and Donna Brown Hogarty. *Parents Magazine*, March 1995.

Scott, Steven. *The Richest Man Who Ever Lived: King Solomon's Secrets to Success, Wealth, and Happiness*. New York: Currency Doubleday, 2006.

Unger, Merrill F. *Unger's Bible Dictionary,* 1985.

*USA Today* (magazine), May 1994, v. 122 n. 2588, p. 9 [1].

*USA Today* (magazine), Jan. 1994, v.122 n. 2584, p. 9 [1].

Washington, Booker T. *Up from Slavery: An Autobiography*.

Webster, Harriet. "Seven Things Smart Parents Never Say." *Readers Digest*, February 1996.

White, Ellen G. *Life Sketches of Ellen G. White.* Mountain View, CA: Pacific Press Publishing Association, 1915.

White, Ellen G. *Reflecting Christ.* Hagerstown, MD: Review and Herald Publishing Association, 1985.

## TEACH Services, Inc.
P U B L I S H I N G

We invite you to view the complete
selection of titles we publish at:
**www.TEACHServices.com**

We encourage you to write us
with your thoughts about this,
or any other book we publish at:
**info@TEACHServices.com**

TEACH Services' titles may be purchased in
bulk quantities for educational, fund-raising,
business, or promotional use.
**bulksales@TEACHServices.com**

Finally, if you are interested in seeing
your own book in print, please contact us at:
**publishing@TEACHServices.com**
We are happy to review your manuscript at no charge.

www.ingramcontent.com/pod-product-compliance
Lightning Source LLC
Chambersburg PA
CBHW070558160426
43199CB00014B/2548